MW00355825

PURTY DANG GOOD

FROM BARTENDER TO BARBECUE TENDER

A TRUE STORY BY
STEVE BURNEY

TABLE OF CONTENTS

For Leni

&

Hannah

&

Kyle

&

Echo

Thank you for putting up with my crazy idea.

It meant the world to me to have each of you along for the ride.

PRELUDE

The seed was planted when I attended a funeral in San Antonio, but I wasn't aware of it then. I had no clue what was coming when I flew in from Seattle to be there for Tom.

Growing up in Texas, we had never been very close. My only brother was seven years older than me. He was of medium height and build with brown eyes and dark wavy hair. Wearing black-framed glasses from an early age, he seemed to develop a personality that was both serious and introverted. On the other hand, I grew to be tall and skinny with blue eyes and light brown straight hair. I developed a personality that was both extroverted and attention-seeking. It's safe to say nobody immediately took us to be brothers. Tom claimed it was because I had been adopted and Mom and Dad were just keeping it from me. He pretty much saw me as an annoying little brat.

As adults we went in completely different directions. He became a certified public accountant. He crunched numbers and got off on reading up on tax codes. Whatever I was, it wasn't about any of that kind of stuff. He married young, just past his twenty-first birthday, with a year to go before he finished college, and even though he worked hard to be a dutiful husband, by the time he was approaching thirty he couldn't escape the realization he was miserable in his marriage. He wanted out. Was it her fault? His fault? No telling; probably a little of both. I wasn't there. I had visions of grandeur. I left Texas at the age of nineteen to go to New York City to chase dreams of being a professional actor. As their marriage played out its real-life drama, I was consumed with myself and my world of make-believe dramas.

When they divorced in the early '80s, it took me by surprise. They had two children and a home, and her side of the family seemed to dote on him. What went wrong? After all the years they'd invested in each other, how could they just pitch it aside like that?

Our own parents had divorced. I was hoping for better for my brother, sister, and myself. It was why I had no interest in being married. All I cared about was finding acting jobs. I had no room for a committed relationship with entanglements that would limit my independence. I liked the idea of being married someday, a day far off in the future. And I didn't want to make the same mistakes my parents had, particularly my father.

He was a train wreck, married at least five times. It might have been six; the final woman he lived with said they were married, but he would neither confirm nor deny it. Neither of them wore a wedding ring. I knew I didn't want to be like him.

After the divorce, my brother left the small town we grew up in and relocated to the closest city, San Antonio. He went through a long period of bachelorhood, his first experience of that as an adult. Sometime later, he met and married a woman named Maggie.

This initially sent shock waves through my sister and me. Maggie brought a nine-year-old girl and her little brother into the marriage. We weren't sure this was a good idea, to marry into an instant family while also having his own young children from the previous marriage to coordinate into the mix. Despite our concerns, Maggie was unfailingly sweet and gracious, and her kids were beyond adorable. We got over ourselves and our reservations.

Their marriage lasted seventeen years, the same length of time our own parents were married, but theirs did not end in divorce. Maggie was having trouble with chronic stomach pain, discomfort, and indigestion. She saw doctors. There were tests to see if she had food allergies, if there was an ulcer, something in her digestive system that wasn't working right. Cancer was not immediately considered. Maggie wasn't a smoker. She had no apparent family history of cancer. She was in her mid-forties and seemed reasonably fit and healthy. The doctor said cancer was a remote possibility.

It was cancer. By the time the diagnosis was certain, the tumor in her stomach had spread to vital organs throughout her body. She fought bravely, but her end was inevitable. Tom stayed in a state of denial throughout, maintaining steadfastly that he would take her home from the hospital and she would be one of the lucky ones God would choose to save. She was too good a person; she did not deserve to be taken before her time in such an unfair way.

Her last days of life were cruel, the disease unrelenting in systematically destroying her body and any resistance to its advance. Her passing was devastating to her children and my brother. Their grief was inconsolable.

When the service concluded and Maggie was lowered into the ground on a cold February day, we closed ranks around Tom and her shattered children, gently urging them, as much as they allowed us, to waiting cars and the long ride home. At the house, we did what families do when they awkwardly try to provide some sense of comfort and normalcy to what is most definitely not comfortable or normal. We ate and drank and made small talk. We tried to be strong.

It was there, watching him keeping his feelings in check and being the polite host, that I felt empathy for my brother.

I wanted, more than I ever had up to that point in my life, to have something in common with Tom, to find a way to build a deeper bond between us, to be a better brother to him than I had been, and to share more of our lives. I just had to figure out how to make that happen. And at that moment, surrounded by sorrow, on a gray, chilly, dreary afternoon in 2004, I was coming up empty.

I was at the beginning of a journey I previously never would have thought possible. I just didn't know it yet.

PART ONE
The History

Before the Idea
1985–2004

CHAPTER ONE
1985–1987

IN 1985, MY ACTRESS girlfriend, Kimberly, who was living with me in New York, decided to return home to Seattle. At the time, we thought we were breaking up, but a year later I gave up trying to make it as an actor and ended up following her to the Northwest. We became engaged, and I thought Seattle might be the right place for us to start our life together. I had always heard nice things about the city, including that there was a vibrant theater scene that I could possibly become involved with.

Then she got pregnant. As her belly grew over the weeks that turned into months, she kept holding me back from making any plans for a wedding. There were more pressing issues we had to deal with first. Primarily, I needed to come up with a decent job. I needed to find a way to make money. There was only one way I thought I might be able to.

"YOU GUYS LOOKING FOR any bartenders?"

The mangy-looking guy behind the bar sized me up for a minute and with a devious smile said, "Yeah, as a matter of fact we are. Hold on a second, let me get the boss. He's in the back."

This was the fifth bar I had walked into along Broadway on Capitol Hill, and it was definitely the seediest-looking of them all. There were no windows letting in light or fresh air, so the room was dark and smelly. Over at a far wall was a big-screen TV playing music videos. That seemed to be the place's biggest draw. Young hipsters had wandered in off the avenue to stand

and gawk at MTV for as long as they could without even trying to order a drink. No one working there seemed to notice or care.

I had worked as a bartender in a bowling alley in Brooklyn when I was a struggling actor, one of many, many survival jobs while pursuing an artistic career. A career that peaked with being cast in a Broadway show that bombed, and then declined into performing children's theater on the road in elementary schools and doing musical theater on the Jersey shore next to a boardwalk carnival arcade.

It was probably fortunate that I started in a bowling alley because I didn't really know what I was doing. I found that even despite that, slinging drinks could include some tips. And if you could get into the right place, the tips could be pretty good. After gaining some experience at the bowling alley, I had enough confidence to talk my way into getting hired in an Upper Eastside nightclub. Besides driving a cab, that was some of the best cash I made in those days.

That cesspool on the corner of Broadway and Denny was my first bartender gig in Seattle. It was a magnet for every oddball, sleazeball, and degenerate in the Capital Hill neighborhood. I worked the day shift Monday through Friday, opening the bar at six o'clock in the morning and withstanding it until two in the afternoon. The regulars arrived from different graveyard shifts. Some were practitioners of overnight street commerce in what could loosely be called the service industry. Others were leftover revelers from the previous night who just didn't know when to stop. The revelers I usually turned around out the door pretty quickly, but the others I just had to tolerate.

The haggard-looking imbibers who lined up before me on the bar stools every morning relentlessly scrutinized my pours with slack-jawed concentration. "Make it a good one, sonny, make it a good one."

Mercifully, I was only there a short time.

One of the regulars was a black guy named Maurice, who worked as a cook at a place called Oscar's. He said they were relocating to a bigger space. The police station was down at the corner, and the owner, Oscar himself, thought moving a little farther away into the Central District might be better for business. They could use another bartender. "A white boy like you could do mighty good there. Whooeee, they'd really take to you."

Maurice set me up to come by to meet Barbara, Oscar's wife. She ran the place. She was a German immigrant Oscar had met and married when he was stationed there about thirty years earlier. She still had an accent. They were the first interracial couple I ever met. Barbara took one look at me and hired me on the spot to be their prime bartender when the new place opened at Twenty-Second Street and Madison Avenue. "You'll do well with us," she said. "Just take care of the house. The regular customers won't give you any trouble, but if they do, I know how to handle them. Take care of the house. If you do that, we'll take good care of you." I was behind the bar six days a week, Tuesday through Saturday, from 6:00 p.m. until closing at 2:00 a.m., and I was working there when my daughter, Hannah, was born.

I rarely saw a white face in the place except Barbara's, and I was sure the novelty of having me there drew in a number of curious neighborhood residents to see me in action, but no one ever was rude or unkind toward me. In fact, after Barbara had spent my first week introducing and presenting me to all her patrons, I was held in high regard. It was like I was appreciated for just being there with them, just treating them politely. The money was decent, though not great. The neighborhood was a little rough, but I always felt safe when I was at work. Nobody wanted any trouble with the police over messing up a white guy.

Then something happened. And Barbara wasn't around to handle it.

It was early in the evening; the crowd wouldn't arrive for another hour. Barbara and Oscar were away at Longacres, playing the ponies, something Barbara was very shrewd at, probably due more to relationships she had made in the paddocks rather than from any innate knowledge of horses. There were maybe a half dozen or so in the place and a couple more at the bar. The waitress was getting drinks from me and bringing them over to tables from time to time.

A man and a woman, both middle-aged, were sitting together at a small table. They had been there most of the afternoon, and I had a suspicion this wasn't the first bar they had stopped at during the day. I was considering cutting them off, never a pleasant prospect, but they weren't bothering anybody, so I served them one more round, which the waitress brought over to them. She put the drinks on the table and waited to be paid. The man said he hadn't ordered the drinks, the woman had. Then she said, "You damn right I ordered 'em. And you gonna pay for 'em. I done bought you three drinks and now you gonna buy. Pay this girl."

He sat rigidly. "I ain't ax't you to buy me drinks. You bought 'em. I drank 'em."

Her eyes narrowed as she started to smolder. "You better pay that girl."

He sniffed. "I think you done drank enough anyway."

The woman leaned in and almost hissed at him. "Are you gonna pay for these drinks?"

The waitress just stood by, shifting nervously from foot to foot.

He shrugged. "I ain't got no money."

Now her eyes opened wide. "You ain't got no money? Bullshit! I know when you ain't got money and I know when you do, and I know for goddamn sure you got plenty. Yo' fuckin' pocket is bulgin' with it!"

He just smiled, revealing yellow teeth. "That ain't money."

She stood up. "You muthafucka! Are you gonna buy these goddamn drinks or not?"

I started to come around the bar. I had to do something. Though I wasn't sure exactly what. But before I could get out from behind it, she reached into a shoulder-strapped handbag on the table and took out a large handgun. I stopped in my tracks.

The waitress dropped her tray and ran screaming into the kitchen. Everyone in the place flew out, streaming through the exit door into the street. I was frozen in terror.

Maurice stuck his head out from the kitchen.

"Get over here! Get down! At least get yo' ass down!" He jerked himself back into the kitchen.

The woman glared at me for a moment, then dismissed me. There were only the three of us in the place. She turned her attention back to the man sitting at the table. He sat perfectly still.

The woman waved her gun at him—it was really a big gun—and then stomped in a little circle around their table, spewing at him, jerking the gun about to punctuate her rant.

"You a cheap, worthless, two-bit, good for nuthin' niggah! You ain't worth shit! You sit on yo' fuckin' ass suckin' down drinks on my money and you ain't even decent enough to treat me like a lady!"

She kept swinging the gun wildly. She didn't have her finger against the trigger; she was holding it by the handle. He didn't respond to her jabbing it at him to make her points. He was motionless, his face frozen in a fixed stare straight ahead.

"You think you can jus' have me anytime you want and I'm s'posed to jus' be grateful fo' yo' sorry ass?" His gaze was straight ahead, not meeting her eyes. "That what you think? Huh?"

She was in front of him again. She glowered at him, but he was implacable. He wouldn't give her anything.

The room was deathly quiet. She stood across the small table from him, her eyes burning into him. He never met her stare, only sat looking straight ahead. Then, finally, her shoulders seemed to relax. The arm with the gun dangled by her side.

The approaching sound of sirens could be heard. They were still off at a distance.

"Shit! I'm too good for you." She paused, sneering at him. "You're not worth the bullet."

She set the gun down on the table, snatched up her handbag, and strode haughtily out of the bar.

The man, still seated, turned and looked at me. He just shook his head and smiled.

I looked at the large gun still lying on the table and took a deep breath. When Barbara got back from the racetrack, I gave her my two weeks' notice.

AFTER THAT, I GOT busy looking for a new job, and got a tip from one of Kim's sisters to check out the downtown hotels because the holiday season was coming on. That was an active time for banquets serving office parties and such. Getting hired on by a hotel, even if it was temporary, could lead to getting my foot in the door of a better gig somewhere else.

I didn't go downtown very much, so I wasn't familiar with where places were. I started at the Westin, when I saw their large towers standing out. I found the Sheraton. I went into the swanky Four Seasons. Everywhere I was handed an application, told to fill it out and bring it back to the front desk, and it would be passed on to the food and beverage director. It was always the same routine and I was feeling like I was banging my head against a wall.

I wandered over by the Bon Marche department store. I thought I might catch the monorail to the Seattle Center, see if the Space Needle was hiring. I passed a discreet opening to an older building, maybe fifteen to twenty stories high, planted on the corner of Fourth Avenue and Olive Way. It had a sign that said, "The Mayflower Park Hotel." It was a little smaller than the other hotels, but I pushed through the double-thick glass doors to take a look inside.

I was in a passageway leading into what looked like a tastefully appointed lobby area, but I didn't reach it because on my left when I walked in was the opening to the bar. A brass-plated sign simply read "Oliver's."

It was fully carpeted. There were marble-topped tables with plush, fancy, dark wicker chairs. Upholstered benches along a wall with smaller variations of the same tables running the entire length of the room. Antique-looking lamps hanging from the walls.

As I came through and went up a couple of steps into the main lounge, I saw a large, ornate crystal chandelier hanging from the middle of the very high ceiling. The wall behind the bar and along the side of the room was made up of a magnificent set of wood-latticed, clear-pane windows, almost from floor to ceiling. One could sit at the bar or some of the tables and have a full view of the people and traffic bustling along outside.

The appearance was one of an immaculately kept room that could have dated back decades. I thought it was the prettiest bar I had ever seen.

"Can I help you?"

I turned around to face a pert, peppy waitress with blond hair neatly pulled away from her face in a ponytail. She was wearing a black, knee-length skirt and a white tuxedo shirt with a black bow tie.

"Hi! I was hoping you guys might be hiring."

She gave me an appraising look. "What kinda job you lookin' for, hot stuff? Not mine, I hope." She was giving me a teasing leer and looked to be eight to ten years younger than me. I wasn't sure if I was supposed to be flattered or insulted.

"I'm a bartender."

She nodded her head. "OK. Greg's in the back room, eating. Let me see if he wants to come out." She walked away and I glanced around the room some more. There were only two guys sitting at the bar. The rest of the place was empty. But it was early afternoon, lunch was over, and happy hour was still a ways off. The two guys had oversize stemmed glasses in front of them that seemed to be martinis. If they were, those were the biggest martinis I'd ever seen. The glasses were practically big enough to be birdbaths.

A guy came out of the back room chewing. He was short and stocky with brown hair and a mustache. He looked to be younger than me, too, about the same as the waitress. "Hi, I'm Greg," he said, swallowing, then taking my hand in a firm grip. "I'm the bar manager. What can I do for you?"

I gave him a rundown of my time in Seattle, getting raised eyebrows when I mentioned the place on Broadway where I started. "You worked there? Jesus, I've been in that bar. What a dump."

"Look, I'll do anything you want: bar back, work banquets, run room service, whatever you need."

"You never worked in a hotel, huh?"

"No, but I'm good with people, and I pick things up pretty quick."

He nodded, sighed, and gazed outside for a moment through the beautiful windows behind the bar. "Can you work tomorrow?"

The hotel was managed by an older married couple who were the principal partners representing a group of silent investors, mostly doctors and lawyers seeking a tax shelter. Mr. Dempsey was an attorney, and he focused on the budget and the bottom line. He cared little about knowing any of the employees. Mrs. Dempsey was the general manager and head of staff. She was the one who personally selected every aspect of the hotel, every design, every detail imaginable.

She was regal in her demeanor, serious and upright, not to be taken lightly. She made it her policy to interview every prospective employee before they were hired. Managers had to run all hiring decisions through her office.

It just so happened that she was out of town when I walked into the hotel. Greg was in a bind and needed another body because they had just lost two guys, who'd quit with no notice. He felt he had to bite the bullet and hire me when I showed up. Mrs. Dempsey was unaware of me.

I started working some events held in the banquet rooms. Greg asked me to work a couple of day shifts in the bar because it was getting busier in the holiday season, with lots of downtown shoppers coming in. I was behind the bar training when Mrs. Dempsey led her managers through the hotel, inspecting every detail and giving orders on what she wanted done.

She took special pride in Oliver's lounge; it was a reflection of her meticulous attention to every aspect of design and style. After resurrecting it, with a complete remodel from its previous sleazy, tacky history as the Carousel Room, she had renamed it Oliver's Lounge, a reference to its location, on the corner of Olive Way. When she saw me, she stopped in her tracks, glaring at me with a scowl from across the room.

"Who is *that*?" she demanded.

Greg rambled on about how he'd needed to make a decision while she was gone. I'd showed up when he needed somebody. I was doing a good job. I seemed like a pretty good guy.

"Well!" she sputtered, shaking her head, "Tell him...to... iron his shirt!" She swept out of the bar with her entourage following behind.

When Greg related what she'd said, I told him she didn't understand.

"This shirt is wash and wear. It says so on the tag. It doesn't need ironing."

He shook his head. "Just do it, man."

CHAPTER TWO
1988–1991

GETTING HIRED AT THE Mayflower was yet another instance of seemingly miraculous events that had occurred throughout my life, as if they had been acts of deliverance by my guardian angel. I had been aware of them since I was a teenager in Texas, brought up as a Southern Baptist, desperately wanting to believe the reason for my being alive was to do something special. At that time, in my callow youth, I thought it had something to do with being a great actor.

When at the age of seventeen my mother and I were washed away with our home in a flash flood and survived an event that took the lives of more than twenty people in our small town, I felt certain that God had to have a Divine purpose for my being on the earth.

At nineteen I went to New York City to prove it, but ultimately, the reality did not turn out the way I had envisioned it. Less than four years after our near-death experience, my mother was snatched away forever in an accident at her home. She slipped in a bathtub and knocked herself out, drowning in the running bath. I was two thousand miles away searching for my Divine purpose.

I was devastated and lost all sense of motivation for what I was doing with my life. I spent less and less time dwelling on why God let me be on the earth, quickly falling away from the faith I had been raised in. However, despite my rebellion and turning away from God, it still seemed like there was some kind of magical safety net that was always there for me.

I lived in New York for ten years, often in vulnerable and even dangerous situations as a cab driver and bartender. I hitchhiked across the country in 1976 and again in 1980, seeking to find some idealized notion of freedom and brotherhood, to prove some theory I wanted to believe in about the innate goodness of people. I went to Ireland in the summer of 1982, wandering the country and searching in vain for some meaning to my existence. Despite repeatedly putting myself in awkward situations that could have had dire, even lethal, consequences, I always came out unscathed.

Getting hired at a classy hotel was a lucky break, but it didn't mean life was going to be easy.

Having a stable job should have made things better. Kim didn't have to worry about me not supporting us. We got through the tough times. We should have been fine. But we weren't. We never got around to getting married, and eventually the subject didn't come up anymore.

Hannah was about fifteen months old the first time we split up. We tried to get back together but kept getting into vicious arguments that broke us up again. I lived in a sublet on Capitol Hill for a couple of months, and then we tried to get back together again. We just found new issues to fight over and finally gave it up for good when Hannah was a little past her third birthday. From then on, I was a weekend dad most of the time. Kimberly and I were both too stubborn and selfish, too caught up in our own grand plans for artistic careers, to put our daughter ahead of all that. I had always sworn I wouldn't do to my own children what my father had done by leaving our family. Instead, I was following directly in his footsteps. I told myself that when the time came that I would actually be married, I would do better. I would make it work for life. I would stay committed through thick or thin.

About a year later word came from my sister, Gerry, that my father was diagnosed with lung cancer and emphysema. The prognosis was grim. He had a few months left, at most.

He owned and operated a couple of trailer parks in Texas, living in one of them close to Austin in a mobile home. I went down for Christmas, bringing Hannah with me so he could see her. He was hooked up to a breathing tube from an oxygen tank. He knew he was doomed. All he could do was sit listlessly in an easy chair with the television on, waiting to die. The trailer he lived in stank of cigarettes from all the years he'd smoked there. Hannah was just a toddler, uncomfortable with nothing familiar to her. She threw tantrums on the floor by his feet while he stared at her impassively. Mostly he ignored her the whole time we were there.

I tried to engage my father in talking to me, hoping we could say some meaningful things to each other, though I wasn't sure what that would be. He didn't show any interest. He was resigned, angry. He was always determined he wouldn't go out in a hospital. He wanted to be home, in his own surroundings. Ultimately, it didn't matter all that much. The suffering was terrible, regardless of where it was.

Tom, Gerry, and I were with him in his trailer at the end. He went into a coma and his breathing became more and more shallow, until his body wouldn't take in any more air. He had run out of fight. It was an ugly way to die, and ugly to watch, but my brother, sister, and I went through it together. We were a family, all we had left. From then on, I had an even deeper appreciation of that.

I'd never intended to be a professional bartender. For many years, I steadfastly held onto the belief that it was only a transitional period of my life. I was doing it to keep bills paid and my life afloat until the time when my real career would happen.

I learned the basics about serving drinks by being around experienced service industry people. I picked up good work habits watching them. The rest was just being there nearly every day, building familiarity, incrementally gaining confidence and knowledge. And, most of the time, behaving as if I knew what I was doing worked for people as much as actually knowing.

That's what I was pretty good at: acting. When I walked behind the bar to start my shift, it was my opening entrance. My audience was lined up before me. Whatever had transpired during the day, if my life was falling apart or I felt like giving up and leaving Seattle, I snapped on a smile along with my wraparound black bow tie and came out to greet my patrons enthusiastically. My coworkers were my supporting actors. My managers were my director and producer. It was showtime until the curtain came down when the bar closed.

My father, in his prime, had a roguish charm. He had a knack for putting people at ease, of engaging them in a friendly, folksy way. My mother, taken from us far too soon in a tragic accident, was a very nice person, but she was more reserved, more serious. Her trademark was perseverance, dedication, commitment. She got up and did what needed to be done regardless of circumstances. She paid the bills.

That was the stock I had come from, and how I evolved into being who I was. I approached being a bartender and everything else I did the same way. I engaged people, put them at ease, and I went to work every single day without fail.

And that was how I met Diane.

During a routine day shift a tall, slender young woman quietly strode in and sat at the end of the bar where she could look out the windows at the people passing outside. She ordered a grasshopper, which struck me as rather odd for a beverage choice during happy hour, but she was nonchalant about it and seemed quite at ease.

I was immediately attracted to her. She had long, thick, wavy brown hair, alabaster skin, and lively blue eyes. After serving her cocktail I lingered after she had given me an appealing smile.

"I haven't seen you here before, have I?"

"No. I came in because I work close by and I'm a little early for my shift."

"Where do you work?"

"I'm at the Camlin Hotel."

"Oh, really? What do you do there?"

"I'm a bartender." She smiled at me again.

"You don't say."

We talked about that for a while, and then I asked her what area she lived in.

"I'm in Wallingford. I have a little rent house with my daughter."

"You have a daughter? I have a daughter, too. She's four."

"Mine will be three at the end of the summer. Her name is Echo." We both pulled out pictures to show each other.

"You know, I live in Wallingford, too. On Latona, between Fortieth and Pacific."

"So do I," she said, her eyes widening.

"No way! I'm in that condo building down toward Pacific."

"I'm two houses below you."

We had never seen each other before. Her name was Diane, and there was an instant spark between us because of the uncanny coincidences in our lives.

I was never one to try to pick up women in the bar. Getting involved with people where you worked, either customers or coworkers, could get very sticky, create awkward situations. One needed to tread carefully on that ground. I wasn't ready to pursue Diane the first time I met her.

Within a week she made a preemptive strike, bringing a girlfriend with her into the bar and sitting at a table within view of me in action. We waved at each other. I caught them glancing at me while I was mixing drinks a couple of times. When I had a moment, I went over to say hi. She suggested I visit her at work sometime. I thought it would be rude if I didn't.

That visit led to a date. The date led to a romance, and before the summer ended I asked her to marry me. She accepted. Because we both had small children and were on the rebound from failed relationships, we decided to keep the wedding private. We only invited a couple of friends as witnesses, and our little girls wore summer dresses.

Diane wanted me to arrange a honeymoon close to Seattle. We needed to keep the cost down and get back to work quickly. I had visited the San Juan Islands in Puget Sound when I was still with Kimberly; one of her brothers ran a charter boat out of Friday Harbor, and he had taken us out around the different islands, which were quaint and beautiful. Diane was from Oregon, part of the Pacific Northwest, so I figured she would appreciate that.

I also wanted to pick someplace neither of us had ever been before, so we could both be seeing it for the first time together, sharing a new experience. I saw on a map that just above the San Juans in Canadian waters were the Gulf Islands. I hadn't previously known they even existed.

The destination I picked was on Mayne Island. I reserved three nights at a bed-and-breakfast. We got there by a combination of driving and taking our car on a ferry. Diane was very quiet; it was hard to get her to hold much of a conversation. Even on the ferry, she mostly just looked out the window without making many comments. We had left the girls with their other parents, and Diane had initially been reluctant to leave Echo in Seattle. It was her first time being apart from her.

The weather wasn't great. We were socked in with a low-hanging haze and intermittent drizzle. It was like that all the way to Mayne Island. The whole trip was close to four hours from Seattle. We drove off the ferry with a couple of other cars onto an island that at first seemed close to uninhabited. There were few buildings, no town to speak of, not many vehicles on the road, not many people in view.

We found the bed-and-breakfast easily. It was nestled in a wooded area just off the road less than five minutes from the ferry. It looked like a large old house, freshly painted and well cared for. We were checked in by a kindly older man with a hint of a clipped British accent in his soft-toned voice. We asked him what kinds of things we might look forward to seeing and doing while visiting the island. He looked rather blankly at us and said, "Some people enjoy fishing," and gave us a courteous smile.

I asked, "Is there something else? A pretty drive, perhaps, with some nice views?"

"Well, what you came in on is our road. You can follow it as far as it goes, a few kilometers or so. Besides that, it's all driveways and gravel roads on private property. There are certainly many trees to see."

Diane said quietly, "Yeah, we've got a lot of those in Oregon, too."

Things weren't starting off with a bang. We took our bags up to the room, which looked like a quaintly decorated spare bedroom in some elderly relative's house. There were laced curtains on a couple of medium-sized windows that looked out over more trees behind the house. Porcelain lamps on small bedside tables. A writing desk. Most of the space was filled with a plush four-poster bed covered with a knitted bedspread over crisp, clean linen sheets.

Diane said, "There's no TV."

"We don't need TV. We're here to be with each other. It'll be fine. Maybe the weather will get better."

"What time is dinner?"

The bed-and-breakfast included a recently converted downstairs room that served as an evening restaurant. It was only open if someone made a reservation. I had made one for us as early as we could be seated.

"They said we could come in at six o'clock."

She looked at her watch. "That's over three and a half hours."

"Yep, that's about right."

"What are we going to do until then?"

I sat down next to her on the bed. "I've got some ideas."

She stood up. "Yeah, well, there's plenty of time for that. I want to do something. Is there anything we can do?"

I looked around the room for a moment. "We could go for a drive."

Three days. The weather never got better, only occasionally worse. We stayed in the room, in the downstairs sitting area, took walks along the road for a few hundred yards. We drove the road once, that first day there. It wound inland away from the waterfront areas. Our host was right: the island had many trees. Not much else. We made the round-trip drive covering the whole island in a little over half an hour. I suggested we make it again on the successive two days we were there, but Diane said that was pointless.

We lingered as long as we could bear it in the dining room at breakfast and dinner. We were served at every meal by the same man who'd checked us in when we arrived. He was always unfailingly polite, asking if we were enjoying our stay and what kinds of things we were doing.

"Oh, we're just looking around," I said. "It's very pretty."

Our host looked at Diane for more elaboration. She just nodded her head, giving him an empty expression.

We only saw three other couples while we were there. They were older, probably retired. The food was well-prepared, but there wasn't much variety. Breakfast was the exact same every time, and we exhausted the choices on the dinner menu. There were mostly different baked fish and steamed vegetables. We tried all the desserts. At least twice.

Finally, I thought the one thing the remote location and the consistently lousy weather allowed for was long, indulgent stretches of time to talk, to learn more about each other, who we really were and how we could more fully understand what was special between us.

That was the rude awakening. I found out we had virtually nothing in common except the similar circumstances in our lives. The more we tried to talk, the more painful it became to keep trying, so we slipped into long, uncomfortable silences. They were silences I would grow to recognize as the most common state between us whenever we were alone together.

It was a shell-shocking experience for me. I didn't want to contemplate that it was anything more than making a horrible choice for our honeymoon destination. There was no way I was going to confront her with any misgivings that could turn the beginning of our marriage into a complete disaster. She obviously felt the same. Neither of us made any mention of how awkward we felt. We both fell into making sarcastic comments about how boring everything was, that the weather was so fitting for such a dead-end kind of a place. When we could finally get up on the third morning and catch the first ferry out, we were as relieved as if we were being released from incarceration.

A week later, we learned she was pregnant.

CHAPTER THREE

1992–1997

THE DEMPSEYS AND THEIR silent partners had bought the hotel at the height of the Boeing bust in the early '70s. It was the time when someone took out a billboard on the highway that said, "Will the last person leaving Seattle please turn out the lights?" They picked it up for a relative bargain.

At that time, the Mayflower Park was primarily a residential hotel with monthly rates. The building and most of the rooms were in serious disrepair. The hotel was built and opened in the '20s, during Prohibition, and the bar area was originally one of the first Bartell drugstores to open downtown.

Then the Great Depression hit. The hotel's owner was heavily leveraged and quickly wiped out. When the drugstore closed years later, the owners of the hotel at that time converted it into a bar. Prohibition was over, but there was a local ordinance that forbade any bar serving cocktails to have windows through which people from the outside could see the patrons partaking in their libations. Thus, wallboard was erected inside and out to cover the wood-paneled windows along the two street-side walls.

The ordinance did not apply to taverns. The thinking was that the predominantly upper-class cocktail drinkers should enjoy some privacy from the prying eyes of the passing riffraff. Taverns, however, with beer-swilling, working-class stiffs as their clientele, should maintain an easier surveillance for paycheck-seeking wives looking to hunt down and corral their wayward spouses.

The first renovation project the Dempseys embarked on was the hotel lobby, but the second, and the one closest to the heart of Mrs. Dempsey, was what she liked to call the lounge. She enjoyed having an evening martini at the end of a long workday, and she wanted a classy bar that would be comfortable and inviting for her and the increasing number of socially emancipated women like her.

During the renovation, quite by accident, the old Bartell windows were discovered, still fully intact. After some investigation, it was learned that the outdated ordinance restricting windows was no longer enforced. Mrs. Dempsey seized on the opportunity and proclaimed her bar would be the first ever in downtown Seattle with windows to look through while enjoying a cocktail.

The transition, from what the bar had been before exposed windows, to what Mrs. Dempsey envisioned it to be after exposing them, was not a particularly smooth process. When the Dempseys took over, the bar was the only part of the hotel showing a profit. It had a steady clientele of waterfront workers, salesmen, and assorted businessmen who worked downtown. The Carousel Room became a haven for ladies of the evening and their pimps, who were typically adorned in flamboyant, fur-collared coats; colorful, plumed, wide-brimmed, face-shadowing hats; and dark sunglasses.

Mrs. Dempsey wanted to establish a new direction that would discourage the unsavory element from dominating her lounge. She imposed a rule that no hats were allowed to be worn in Oliver's. They had to be removed before anyone could be served. No sunglasses either. Off-duty police officers were hired as security guards to enforce the new restrictions and serve as a deterrent to any efforts at using the hotel, and especially its bar, for illicit purposes. The pimps took their business elsewhere.

When I came on the scene more than a decade later, the only remnants of those wild days were the off-duty cops still nonchalantly cruising through in the evening from time to time. I still was not supposed to let anyone wear hats, but by the time I was running the bar it had pretty much become a joke.

The pimp hats had given way to a young generation of guys wearing baseball caps and girls with berets.

The other hang-on from the old days were the gargantuan, oversize cocktail glasses, used mostly for martinis. When I started there, I was taught a method of premixing martinis by filling plastic gallon jugs with gin, cut with water and vermouth. I'd fill another one the same way with vodka, and another with bourbon. These were what they used for their house martinis and Manhattans. They were double-size and cheap, like the ingredients used in making them.

Going into the '90s, Mrs. Dempsey was ready to step down from leading the day-to-day management of the hotel. She wasn't going away—she would still be a looming presence, casting a discerning eye over all she had painstakingly created—but she was ready to install a general manager to handle the operational tedium.

Mark Novac started as the food and beverage manager while Mrs. Dempsey groomed him to take over the top job. He was all custom-tailored suits with stylish ties, and had closely cropped salt-and-pepper hair with a matching manicured mustache. He looked like a regular client of the Gene Juarez hair salon where Seattle's upper crust went to be clipped and pampered.

He took one look at me making plastic jugs of premixed martinis and grimaced.

"You cannot be serious," he blurted out.

"Hey, we got a bar full of regulars who come in and pound these things daily. It's gotta be the best bang for the buck in all of downtown. We got one guy alone, big guy in a business suit, who puts down six or seven Manhattans damn near every day. He has a regular table we hold for him and his friends."

Novac shook his head.

"How much do you put into those ridiculous-looking glasses?"

"I think they hold twelve ounces. We put in maybe eight. Well, maybe nine or so."

"And these people are able to walk out of here without stumbling?"

I was starting to feel a little put on the spot.

"Uh, well...yeah...I mean...they're pretty conditioned to it. Sometimes it can be a problem, I guess. We try to keep a handle on it. It's just...we're kinda known for these big martinis. It's what a lot of our regulars come here for. It's been this way forever."

He gave a last, disgusted look at the plastic jug of generic rotgut.

"Well, things are going to change."

AFTER DIANE AND I married we moved into a rental house, an old, two-story, red-brick Tudor in the Wallingford neighborhood, near Greenlake. It was almost a hundred years old with a full, concrete- walled basement and a detached, one-car garage that backed out directly onto the street. The owner, a Boeing engineer approaching retirement age, had inherited it from his parents. He was fine with renting it to us for a year, but his ultimate goal was to sell it when he could fetch the price he had in mind for himself.

In the spring we had a baby boy and named him Kyle. Our girls were excited because they had a baby brother to ogle. They couldn't wait until he got big enough to get their hands on him. He was the best doll ever.

Diane had a new baby to dote on and I had a son to look forward to playing with. I imagined us playing catch, watching football together, going to the park and chasing each other around, maybe getting a dog.

Of course, I could have done these things, and to some extent had, with Hannah and Echo, but it's just not the same feeling as looking forward to doing it with your son. My own father left when I was five years old. Tom wasn't one to play with me much back then. I did all right. I found neighborhood kids to play with, roam around and do things with. But I never really had a dad.

I learned to pitch a baseball with Dane Hebert and his dad in their backyard. I learned to ride a bike with Terry Galleon's dad. I learned about model trains and that root beer could be made at home with George, my next-door neighbor. George was a newlywed, and when he and his pregnant wife moved away to a larger house in a different part of town, I cried.

Now I could make it different for my son. I could be with him every step of the way. I wanted that for him, but I wanted it even more for myself. I didn't want to be my father. I swore I would never do that to my children. I would be different.

The new general manager, Mark Novac, was shaking things up at work. He was laying down new policies and procedures, much to the resentment of the staff. He was being strict with uniform code and proper grooming, forcing out those he felt weren't team players.

Fortunately, I hadn't landed on his bad side. I had seniority of the bartenders and my boss was satisfied that I was managing the bar well on my night shifts. But the new GM was changing the way we served drinks, limiting the amount of drinks we could sell to each customer. Our regulars, especially at happy hour, were becoming irate and started looking for other bars to hang out at.

Novac was fine with that. He said we were going to completely change our image. He said to have patience and the staff would see things get better again, much better. Most of us went along with the program, though a couple of employees did move on. I felt I had no choice. The chances of getting a comparable job that provided health insurance benefits and paid vacations were nonexistent. If I did anything that caused me to lose this job, I didn't want to imagine how Diane would react. So, I kept my head down and played by all the rules.

It was in the first summer we had Kyle that I broached the subject with her of going back to school. After breaking up with Kimberly a couple years earlier I had started taking classes at the community college, eventually transferring to the University of Washington with the goal of getting a teaching certificate. I thought I might make a decent English/drama teacher someday. I had to put those plans on hold when she had become pregnant, but now we were getting more settled.

"I think I can look at starting up again in the fall quarter. We seem to be getting a good routine down. I could just go part-time, maybe two classes. I think I could work out a schedule where I wouldn't leave you stuck too much without help."

She didn't respond.

"So, whatta ya think? You got a problem with that?"

She started slowly, quietly. "I have some thoughts about going to school, too."

"Uh-huh?"

"There's a nursing program at North Seattle Community College. I'd have to spend some quarters getting my requirement courses to transfer to a full RN program later on, but I think I could complete it in three or four years."

"Nursing? You want to be a nurse?"

"Well, it's not like it's some life ambition or something. But next year I'll be thirty. I need to start thinking about the future. Nobody wants to see a woman getting old and losing her looks behind a bar. But being a nurse is something I can do when I'm old, until I want to retire even."

"OK."

"It's a really good job. It pays great, even better than what I can make now. It's got great benefits, health insurance that will cover the kids."

"Yeah, nurses make good money, and there's lots of demand."

"Exactly. Me being a nurse is just so much more practical. I mean, what do teachers make? Not much, right? You probably do better just working the job you already have."

"Well, it's not really about that."

"Men can be bartenders forever. Nobody cares if you get old; it makes you distinguished. Women just look gross."

"I don't think old men look particularly better behind a bar."

"I would like to think I wouldn't have to deal with drunks coming on to me forever. Why not do something I can do until I retire that would pay well and not have me breathing secondhand smoke and pretending to be nice to sleazeballs so they might leave me a decent tip?"

"I understand. I get it. I never wanted to be a bartender for the rest of my life either."

We cobbled together a compromise where we both went to school part-time. She had a morning class, and I went in the afternoon. We both went to work in the evening. We saw each other only if the other one was awake when we got home after closing at two in the morning.

When I got my bachelor's degree, I didn't attend the graduation ceremony. It wasn't even noted, except for my receiving my diploma in the mail.

I never spoke of going on to get a teaching certificate. I didn't really have any thoughts about being a teacher or an actor anymore. I was a bartender. It's what I had been for years. I was over forty years old. It was silly to think I'd ever be anything else. I got the degree. It was what my mother had wanted for her children. I stuck it out and finished, mostly in her honor.

Seattle was in a boom period during the '90s and real estate prices were climbing. Our landlord told us he was putting the house on the market and we would likely have to move. I was done with school, so I started searching to see if we could buy a house of our own. It looked like with our combined incomes, we could qualify for something, maybe in the suburbs.

I found an old, run-down rambler in the suburb of Shoreline, with a big, fenced backyard. I could see myself playing catch back there someday with my son. We made an offer and got it. There were lots of kids on the block, and soon our girls had friends to play with.

Diane threw herself into school. She worked the weekend nights and I worked the weekday nights; that way we didn't need sitters anymore. We were both pretending we were busy with our home and children, with our jobs and her going to school. Busy, busy, busy.

The '90s should have been the happiest years of my life. I was married, I had sweet, innocent children, I had a home. Everything was there, but none of the pieces fit. It was a string of years when all that mattered was going to work and paying the bills and getting everybody where they needed to be every day. Diane and I just grew further and further apart.

She got her certificate and had her first job lined up. She left behind being a hotel bartender for good. We stayed together another few months, but we were honest with each other that we were only doing it for the children. She was the one to say that wasn't a good enough reason, that it was better for them if we tried to live our lives with a hope of being happy instead of having them watch their parents live together miserably. I felt she was probably right.

I eventually agreed to divorce and move out into an apartment nearby. I took Kyle to a park and, sitting on swings next to each other, I tried to break it to him gently that Daddy wasn't going to be living with them anymore. Kyle nodded his head, but didn't seem to really understand what his dad was talking about. After all, he was only five years old. The same age I was when my father left. I had become the man I always swore I never wanted to be.

CHAPTER FOUR
1998–2001

I ALWAYS SAID TOM and I had nothing in common. Now we did. We'd both divorced our first wives. Neither of us liked to talk about it. We weren't prone to having talks together about our feelings.

I saw my brother rebuild his life, transcend his previous circumstances, and come out of it with a new marriage that was strong and fulfilling. He and Maggie were married for over a decade when I divorced Diane. They were clearly going to spend the rest of their lives together, married to each other.

Now I was the loser, the one who couldn't make marriage work. Tom and Gerry had family dinners, family vacations, family pets, family friendships. I lived by myself in an apartment, had visitation rights, two separate child support payments. I rarely had visitors besides my children. When I ate at home it was usually alone, mostly frozen dinners or a sandwich. I was in my forties and couldn't imagine ever being attractive to anyone else again.

I took an apartment that was only five minutes away when I broke up with Diane. It was a one-bedroom, but I got a nice convertible couch that the kids could sleep on when they were with me. The thing that sold me on being there was an indoor pool in the front of the building. I knew the kids would really enjoy that.

I took them to Texas with me once a year in the summer. We went to South Padre Island for some family vacations. I was able to bring Echo with us a couple of times as well. It felt good to have them play with Tom and Gerry's kids, even though my kids were much younger. I wanted them to have a connection to my family, despite living so far apart in the Northwest. I wanted them to feel like they belonged.

"YOU'VE GOT MAIL!"

I got a new Dell desktop computer that included a CD-ROM for a subscription to America Online. The internet beckoned like a siren. There were people I could connect with in chat rooms, in forums, playing games, through email and instant messaging.

A home page gave me the latest news, sports, and weather reports. Everything I needed was right there in front of me and responded to my desires by the simple click of a mouse. I spent hours online when I was home alone. I spent hours when my kids were with me after they were asleep. I loved talking anonymously to others, or sometimes just following them talking to one another, about sports, or traveling, or relationships. I saw personal ads on Love.com from women looking to find someone to meet, to become involved with.

I was ravenous at looking at the ads, imagining a response, making contact. But I didn't take action. I wasn't ready to do that. It seemed a little weird, desperate. If I met someone, I wanted it to be more natural, more of an instant, mutual attraction. Love at first sight. Or at least at sight, whatever number of times it took. Hooking up with strangers online just seemed like a game for lonely hearts, for losers. No way I was ever going to do that. No way.

During the '90s, Oliver's evolved into an environment more fitting to the tasteful decor Mrs. Dempsey had labored to create. Early in the decade we went through a series of renovations that brought new carpet, new window dressings and draperies, fresh paint throughout, reupholstered chairs and benches, rebuffed marble-top tables and bar counter. The crystal chandelier was painstakingly disassembled and deep cleaned, panel by panel.

When it was all done, the bar glistened with sophistication. The bird-bath cocktail glasses were abandoned at the price of driving away most of the regulars who were dedicated to them, and replaced with delicate, tapering glasses that held about a third as much volume as their predecessors.

The cheap, generic product we previously used was replaced with higher-profile call brands. The managers developed recipes for specialty cocktails using fresh and more exotic ingredients, shopping at the Pike Place Market for things like locally grown raspberries, blueberries, ginger root, and kumquats. Each cocktail was individually prepared and garnished to provide maximum visual appeal, as well as a tasty flavor.

The martinis were given special emphasis, vigorously shaken and strained into a chilled glass with shards of ice crystals rising to the top, exuding frosty temptation. Plump Spanish olives were used for a garnish, or else a long, thin twist of lemon taken directly from the rind for each serving. It became all about class and presentation.

Mark Novac came up with a marketing idea he enlisted three other bars to join in on, something called the Seattle Martini Challenge. He was very calculating in recruiting three bars that were regarded as among the finest in the city: the Hunt Club in the Sorrento, the downtown Westin, and the poshest of all, the Palm Court at the Four Seasons Olympic.

The plan was simple enough: the event would be a one-evening extravaganza. A panel of nine judges—each location had at least that many stools at their bar—would be recruited from local celebrities, television and radio on-air personalities, or newspaper and magazine feature writers. They would ride in limos to each location, whisked in like royalty to a featured position at the bar from which they were to be served three items. One would be a classic martini served straight up. Another was a specialty cocktail, also served straight up, that could contain any ingredients as long as its primary one was gin or vodka. The third was an appetizer designed to be the perfect complement to the two cocktails.

The final destination was to be Oliver's. After their presentation and a brief period of deliberation, everyone retreated across from the bar to an upstairs banquet area that overlooked the hotel lobby. There they found an offering of heaping appetizers and two banquet bars freely dispensing wine, beer, and the specialty cocktails and martinis served in the competition.

After the party, at which the grand announcements were made for the winning bar in each category, the judges could retire at their leisure to complimentary rooms provided for them to recover from the efforts of drinking at four different bars and then toasting one another multiple times at the party. In the morning they were welcomed into the hotel restaurant for breakfast on the house and then sent on their way with gift baskets.

It worked like a charm. Recruiting judges was a cinch. It guaranteed coverage by the local press and broadcast media. All the judges dressed in vintage, or else elegantly dashing, attire, as did most of the entourage of media and industry followers who trailed them. Each bar had its opportunity to shine in the spotlight, providing the finest they could concoct and design for discriminating palates.

As the judges arrived at each location, the crowd following them increased, until, when they swept triumphantly and tipsily into Oliver's, the place was packed shoulder to shoulder. TV cameras cast their bright lights over the throng. Columnists jotted their notes for future weekend editions. The attention and coverage were priceless.

That first year Oliver's got skunked. The Four Seasons swept the awards. The other two hotels felt it was a silly boondoggle and rigged against them and would never participate again. It didn't matter. Being seen on a par with the image and clientele of the Four Seasons was enough to make the Dempseys ecstatic. The spectacle would be an annual affair. The next year the two new players were highly respected downtown restaurants with top bartenders, the Metropolitan Grill and Il Bistro. The latter featured perhaps the most renowned bartender in Seattle, Murray the Blur. He was legendary in his knowledge, his technique, his discretion. He was a consummate professional.

That second year the judges started to figure out who was making the party possible. The other places were just agreeing to participate, but it was the Mayflower Park that produced the entire experience for everyone. The

Four Seasons was the big winner again, except this time one award came to Oliver's. The one for the best classic martini. It was exactly the one Mrs. Dempsey coveted.

Murray the Blur was shut out even though industry professionals touted him as incomparable. Il Bistro, and Murray, would never play that game again. The word started spreading in the business that it was all just a self-serving vanity show. The Dempseys didn't care. They continued making upgrades in the hotel, and they steadily increased the prices.

There was a phenomenon occurring in Seattle as the '90s progressed, increasingly taking hold with each annual Martini Challenge. The internet was growing exponentially inside desktop computers in every home. Businesses were rushing to find ways to join in on the expected innovations that people would embrace by using their computers to do things, and buy things, that they hadn't even thought about before. Dot-com was the new buzzword.

New internet businesses were popping up downtown and on the east side close to Microsoft. Young people fresh out of college were getting into start-up companies on the ground floor, receiving stock options as part of their benefits. And the stock market was soaring. The feeling was that the world was changing at a dizzying pace.

And old things were cool again. Like martinis and sweet cocktails like cosmopolitans and lemon drops. Every year the Martini Challenge appealed to a new wave of young urban professionals, and every year Oliver's kept being awarded the prize for having the best classic martini in Seattle. When asked how to explain our dominance in always winning that category, I usually shrugged and said, "Being the last drink the judges have doesn't hurt. By that time, it's probably the only one they can remember."

We rode that wave all the way through the decade, but as the new millennium approached, there were changes we had to adjust to. Mark Novac was offered a position at another hotel that appealed to him and he left, followed out the door shortly thereafter by his food and beverage manager. When Paul Ishii and Steve Johansson were installed in those positions and expected to maintain the high level of achievement in the Martini Challenge, they looked around and saw me as the most experienced participant of it. They asked me to take on the job of being bar manager, and I led the staff to plan for the next Challenge.

We held on to the trophy for the best classic martini one more year. But the party was over. That same year, the dot-com bubble burst. There was some talk of maybe trying to resurrect the Challenge after taking a break, but it never came to pass, and after multiple dot-coms downtown going under, the Seattle Martini Challenge was as lost as the Roaring '20s when the Great Depression hit. It was a hell of a good time while it lasted.

After the Seattle Martini Challenge was out of the picture, Paul Ishii asked me to take on managing the restaurant, Andaluca, as well as Oliver's. The Mediterranean-style restaurant had burned through three restaurant managers in less than a year. They each left because of continuous friction with a new chef and longtime servers behaving like prima donnas. Paul thought I might have better luck because I was well-liked by all the food and beverage staff. I also was loyal to the hotel. I was a team player.

Because two manager positions were being combined into one, the new responsibilities also came with a substantial pay raise. I was surprised to learn that my increased income could qualify me for a mortgage in buying a modest house in Shoreline. I received this information from Hannah's aunt Lynne, Kim's sister, a hotshot real estate agent.

"But I have two child support payments."

"That doesn't have to be disclosed in your liabilities."

"Why not?"

"It's discriminatory. They only look at your consumer debt. Is your car paid off?"

"Yeah."

"Do you have student loans? Credit card debt?"

"No. I got grants for school. I passed on the loans that were offered. And I pay off my credit card balance every month." Just like my mother would have taught me to, if she had lived long enough to see credit cards fully evolve. My memory from childhood was of her sitting down at the kitchen table once a month with her large, three-ring checkbook binder. She dutifully wrote out each check as she worked through her collected stack of monthly bills, placing them in envelopes that were neatly set aside to be mailed in a timely fashion.

That was her monthly ritual, her victory of independence, her proof to herself that she could keep things normal for her children, that they were fine for another month.

So, I bought a house. It was an old house, but it was in pretty good shape. Hannah and Kyle would have their own bedrooms. The backyard was fenced. Kyle and I could play catch there.

Even though I had the responsibility of owning a house, even though my life was consumed with working and being a dad, even though I had a position that could someday lead to becoming the food and beverage manager of the entire hotel, I still let myself dream sometimes that I could be an actor someday. That was truly the only profession I had ever aspired to in my life, what I had set out to be when I left my mother's house to go to New York City as a teenager.

It was so long ago, so much had happened, and so much of it unexpected. I was in my mid-forties and doing what I felt obligated to do, not what I felt was in my heart to do. I had always wanted to believe, as I had often been told along the way, that anything could be achieved if you just set your mind to it and stayed committed to working at it. Dreams could come true. You just had to keep believing in them and never give up.

But it had all gone so woefully wrong.

How could I expect to be a role model for my children when I couldn't even make it work with either of their mothers? How could I set an example for them when I wasn't doing anything in my life I really wanted to do, only what seemed the responsible thing, the most practical. I was living exactly the kind of life I had fled Texas to avoid. I wanted a life that was full of creativity and passion, of artistic expression. Instead, I was a servant. I made a living being a good steward and taking care of Mr. and Mrs. Dempsey's hotel, their family business, their dream. Not my own.

So, I kept looking at what the Seattle theaters were doing, looking on the internet at sites that showed where auditions were happening, what kinds of classes and workshops were going on, where I could get a foot in the door to be cast in a play, to be an actor again. Mostly, though, I just entertained fantasies about it.

I did give myself some credit for making the best of things. I liked owning a house. I liked paying my exes regularly and living up to my responsibilities. I appreciated being involved with my children and having them with me as often as I could. But I wasn't living the life I had once imagined for myself, and that bothered me.

CHAPTER FIVE
2001

I WAS EARLY, AS usual. I hated being late for anything. Tardiness was rude, disrespectful. I am always impressed, and slightly surprised, when others seemed to treat their appointments the same way I do.

Standing on the pathway, looking over the placid city lake before me, the warm daylight was giving way to a comfortable spring evening. Curious ducks with muted squawks paddled close to the shore, expecting bits of bread or other food to be thrown in for them to race one another and peck at. More ducks and a swan, seeing the initial ones gathering, started moving in to join them, but as I only stood without offering any treats to hold their attention, they all drifted away, their quacks falling off into quiet gliding detachment.

Sorry, guys, I thought as I watched them disperse, *I'll probably be coming up empty, too.*

Even though I had scoffed at the idea of internet dating, weeks of being alone stretched into months. Increasing desperation propelled me to stick my toe in the water.

Greenlake was a good meeting place. The small lake was a haven for urban exercise, its less-than-three-mile circumference traversed by runners, walkers, people on Rollerblades, bicyclists, skateboarders, dog walkers, baby strollers, and the occasional unicyclist. There were ample park benches along the path to sit and people-watch. It allowed for anonymous privacy within a very public setting.

This was much better than the typical places I made my internet date rendezvouses. Usually someplace downtown. A nice bar, not the one I worked at, with a restaurant either attached or close by. The first time I had started with the commitment of having dinner. That proved unfortunate, as I knew upon the initial greeting that all I wanted to do was escape at the earliest opportunity.

She was a career woman working in high technology for Paul Allen's company, Vulcan Real Estate. I sat through cocktails and then a long, long, long evening, listening to my date insist that she was "just a regular gal" who didn't think herself more special than anybody else. We ended the evening outside the restaurant with a polite handshake as her BMW was being brought up by the valet.

So, the next time I made the date just for drinks. The peroxide blonde in the too-tight dress wearing too much makeup gulped too many cosmopolitans while interjecting throughout her life story:

"Oh my God, I never do this kind of thing!"

And then, later, "This is so not me. It's so funny to be doing this!"

And then later, with slurry bravado, "Well, I guess this wasn't too bad. I could probably do it again."

I couldn't. Finally, she had enough drinks in her that I was able to pour her into a cab.

So, the next time I made the date for coffee in a neighborhood cafe that didn't serve alcohol.

The petite, frizzy-haired woman was sitting waiting for me in a corner booth, immediately devouring me on sight with yearning, desperate, unrequited desire. I knew equally immediately I had no interest, but I stayed with her almost an hour because doing otherwise felt cruel. She hunted exhaustively to find some common ground between us, an opening, something that might bind us in shared interest to build on toward developing a connection.

When I shook her hand in parting, she clutched it and had a hard time letting go until I gently pulled it away.

So, the next time, this time, I made the date to meet at Greenlake.

What am I doing here? I thought dejectedly. *This is such a loser's game. My God, how humiliated I would be for anybody I know to see me right now. Standing here like some doofus, expecting that something this desperate could really work.*

"Hello?"

I turned around. "Oh, hi! Are you Leni?" I instinctively put out my hand and she took it. Hers was warm and soft. As I looked into her eyes, I thought, *OK. This is good. Maybe.*

"I'm not late, am I? Have you been waiting long?"

"No, no, I was early." I glanced at my watch. "You're right on time." I smiled. "Right on time."

"Good. Well, I hate to be late."

"Yeah, I know, me too." I was staring at her. I should probably stop doing that. "Uh, you want to walk a bit? Find a place to sit?"

We started down the pathway with joggers and bikers passing us in both directions. The passing throng could have been a parade of movie stars. I was only conscious of her. She was the right height, not too tall or too short. She was the right size, not too heavy or too skinny. She was the right age, not much younger or older than me. She was wearing white shorts that showed her to have shapely legs, but she wasn't dressed in any way that was trying to be sexy or younger than she was. She talked easily with me but didn't come off trying to be anything or anyone she wasn't, or what she might think I expected her to be. She was real.

We found a bench along the pathway that seemed cozy, where we could sit together and observe both the lake and the people passing as we exchanged our stories, stories that had similarities and differences.

Like me, she was divorced. She had spent her entire adult life as a housewife, living in the country, rarely venturing into the city. I had spent my entire adult life living in cities, rarely finding myself in the country. We both agreed that just a few years earlier, before the internet, there was little chance we would have found ourselves sitting together gazing out over Greenlake.

After her divorce, she tried to reinvent herself by starting a late career as a flight attendant. She enjoyed the opportunity to travel and see different places, but the constant grind of in-flight service, the takeoffs and landings, the choppy, bumpy trips over the mountains, the fogginess of waking up not sure where she was or where she was going until she blinked her eyes around another strange, unfamiliar hotel room and thought about it…that was beginning to wear on her more than it did the generally younger flight crews she worked with. She was starting to feel like it would be nice putting down some kind of roots again. Though she wasn't sure how or what that might look like.

We sat together as daylight faded into the oncoming evening, the time melting away with easy conversation. I knew, as the darkness was coming, that we were going separate ways, so I asked if she would like to see me again.

"Yes," she said shyly, looking away from me toward the lake. "That would be nice."

I moved closer to her and was only inches away when I whispered, "Can I kiss you?"

She looked surprised and pleased, and I sensed she was feeling awkward, like a schoolgirl.

"OK," she murmured.

I moved slowly, not wanting to make it anything more than something tender, sincere, a connection. We held our kiss for a long moment, and when our lips parted and our eyes met, I believed I had once again found hope.

We dated steadily through the spring and summer. She became familiar with my modest house, appraising it approvingly, as if making mental notes of all the feminine improvements she could make in every room and in the yard outside as well. I became familiar with the small, country apartment she rented in a converted barn loft on a farm south of Seattle, far from even the fringe of the city but still an easy commute to the airport for work.

We weren't too much in each other's faces because I had my steady job at the hotel, and Leni was often away, flying on three- or four-day trips.

We held off on meeting each other's children. Hers were fully grown adults and bitter toward her for giving up on their father. They were appalled at the thought of her being involved with any other man, let alone some hotel manager, a glorified servant.

My children were too young to have much awareness of me as a person. I was protective of imposing another adult female on them, or forcing them to accept her as some new mother figure in their father's house. It was already plenty challenging for them, having separate mothers of their own.

So, the intimate dance of moving toward a deeper relationship played on for us until the summer passed and my children settled back into school. I could sense that we were approaching a crossroads in our relationship; it would either continue on a path of deepening commitment leading toward an inevitable remarriage, or in a direction that would probably have us go our separate ways. Having her meet my children, or me hers, could not be put off much longer.

I was slowly coming around to accepting that Leni was a good woman I should feel lucky to have come into my life. She was sweet and caring and generous and completely ready to be committed to me. I started feeling like the direction we were moving in was natural, maybe even God or Fate working in both of us, steering us toward reclaiming and rebuilding our lives together. I kept insisting to myself that any feelings of doubt or hesitation were just my fear, just feeling gun-shy because of the misfires in the past. At our age, this time it didn't have to be so much about our children.

That's where my mindset was right up to the morning I got up, like I always did, to get ready to go to work. I turned on my computer and logged on, like I always did, to check for emails, mostly from Leni, and to glance at my homepage for the day's news, sports, and weather. The date was September 11.

CHAPTER SIX

2001–2003

I DUMPED HER. I dropped Leni like she was a real estate agent I changed my mind about after listing my house with her. It took me six weeks to do it because she hadn't done anything to deserve it. It was me, all me. Watching those jets flying into the Twin Towers changed everything.

I'd looked out from the observation deck of those magnificent buildings on several occasions, the expanse of Manhattan stretching before me. I had taken high school students up there as a tour guide in my struggling actor days. I had stood outside at the base in the plaza, craning my neck to peer up at the massive structure, the two of them seeming like invincible sentinels of the American dream.

And now they were gone. I watched them collapse, first one and then the other. I saw it on the internet. It didn't seem real. I couldn't comprehend it. Nowhere was safe. America wasn't safe anymore.

Something was deeply shaken inside me. I just couldn't cope with the shock and grief, and then will my life to go back to being normal. Life was fragile. It was precious. It could be gone in an instant. There was no time to lose.

I changed. My feelings changed. I couldn't commit to Leni. I didn't want to be trapped in a relationship or another marriage just because I was lonely. I didn't want to get stuck on a path that would keep me working at the hotel for the rest of my life. I wanted to bust loose. I wanted to live the kind of life I had imagined myself living since the first time I played a character on a stage in front of an audience.

I didn't rush into anything. I knew I was rattled. Maybe it was temporary. Maybe I would wake up from it like a bad dream. I kept going to work. I kept seeing Leni, being with her, acting like things were the same. Maybe it would pass.

Three weeks after my world changed forever, Tom and Maggie came to town. Maggie worked for a giant insurance company based in San Antonio. She was given an achievement award and invited to attend an honorary dinner in Seattle for her and other employees also being recognized. Everything was at the company's expense for her and her husband.

I set them up to stay at the Mayflower and took them to see the usual tourist spots. Pike Place Market, the waterfront, a ferry ride to Bainbridge Island, the Space Needle. I arranged for them to have dinner in Andaluca. I invited Leni so I could introduce her. Tom and Maggie were wonderful to her, made her feel like she was already part of the family. Leni did everything she could to look nice and give them a favorable impression of her. All of them commented on the tasty Mediterranean food and the stylish ambiance of the restaurant. By all appearances, the dinner was a great success. Tom and Maggie went back to Texas and Leni believed she had passed the first test of meeting family approval.

But I was miserable. Nothing felt right. I couldn't make a life with Leni. I didn't know how to explain it to her. It wasn't about her.

Finally, with Thanksgiving coming on and Christmas to quickly follow, I knew I had to rip off the Band-Aid. Leni was starting to make overtures about meeting children, both mine and hers. About dinner invitations, gift ideas, holiday events. It was time to fully reveal ourselves as a couple.

I broke up with her the same way I met her, with an email. She was blindsided, never saw it coming, couldn't believe it at first. She responded to me with her own email, begging me to explain what had happened, what had she done, what was wrong. I couldn't really want to break up, just like that, for no reason except that I just didn't think it could work. What about all we had done together, all the intimate time we'd spent together? I couldn't just end it all without making her understand why.

Then she got angry. She sent me a flaming torch in an email, saying that I was obviously tired of her and was now ready to move on to someone new. I was bored.

She was glad to be done with me. I was a fake and a phony and had used her and then tossed her aside. I was a pig, like most men were, no different. I didn't deserve her or any decent woman and she was well rid of me.

I took it all. She was right. And I felt awful about it. But I also felt it was what I had to do.

In the summer I took my kids to Texas for a wedding. Gerry's daughter, Stacy, was getting married. Stacy had been up in Seattle as an intern for Microsoft after getting out of MIT. She and Hannah had grown close through the years, mostly during family vacations at South Padre Island. Even though Hannah was only a teenager at fifteen, Stacy wanted her as one of her bridesmaids. She wanted me to recite some scripture passages as part of the ceremony in my best dramatic style.

The young man she was marrying came from a good family in Pennsylvania. They'd met at school and both had bright futures before them. They understood technology; not just how to use it, but what its potential was, what its future could be. They understood it as a business, as a tool to be leveraged for their professional advancement. It was like they were perfectly fluent in a language people like me were struggling to learn a few conversational phrases of.

I had been nothing like them at their age. Not even close.

Tom and Maggie were surprised I'd broken up with Leni. They'd expected me to bring her to the wedding. What had happened? She had seemed so nice, so interesting, with so many stories of flying around to different places. It was a shame it didn't work out.

That always seemed to be the theme for me with my family. Things just didn't work out. The promising auditions, finally getting cast in a Broadway play, making a career as an actor in New York. None of it came to anything. That was a shame. Moving to Seattle to be with Kimberly, being married to Diane, now this breakup with Leni. All of them down the drain. That was too bad. Sorry to hear it. And then the pep talk. You'll be OK. Things will work out. You still have a lot to be grateful for. Life's never what we expect it to be. You've got too much going for you to not be with someone soon. You're still a good catch.

But I was feeling like that train had left the station.

THE DEMPSEYS ALWAYS REWARDED their employees with a party in January, after the busy holiday season was over. The hotel was intensely busy during that time of year, especially Oliver's, because of its windows looking out over the bustling sidewalks outside. Being divorced, I worked every holiday, teasing the customers that I was commiserating with the other lonely hearts like me, who had no place else to go.

I brought the kids, including Echo, to the employee party, where the girls clamored to entertain everyone with songs at the rented karaoke machine. There was food and drinks and desserts and lots of prizes given away in a raffle that all the employees were entered in.

My name was picked for one of the prizes. I won a two-night stay at one of the better hotels in Vancouver. The kids were beside themselves with excitement. They wanted to go see Vancouver, too. It wasn't like I had anybody to make it a romantic getaway with, so I decided it would make a nice road trip. I made weekend reservations for us to drive up there.

We stayed in the city, went to Granville Island, spent some time in Stanley Park, ate Chinese food, swam in the hotel's indoor pool, watched movies in the room. I enjoyed the feeling of having them with me, having them close. The world and its problems seemed to disappear for a while.

On the drive back to Seattle down I-5, my mind drifted into thinking about my children, staying involved with them. They liked my work, the things my work had allowed them to do. It wouldn't be too very long before Hannah would want to seek her first job somewhere, with hopes of getting her first car, her own spending money, her independence.

What if I could get her a job at the hotel? I could probably arrange that. Maybe even Echo a couple of years behind her. It was possible, I supposed.

A roadside sign indicated the next exit had food and gas available. One of the food places was Subway. I liked Subway. It was fast, easy. The sandwiches were good. The kids would eat it. I decided to pull in and have a bite to eat.

I sat, chewing my sandwich, looking around, the kids doing the same in the booth with me. I thought about where we were. Subway. It was a franchise. I looked at the young people behind the counter. I could see it. What if I owned a Subway? What if I could give my kids jobs there, each one of them as they became old enough? There weren't any Subways at that time in my area of Shoreline. I wondered what it cost to own a franchise. I could leave the hotel. I could be my own boss. I could provide an opportunity for my kids that would keep me closely involved with them the whole time they were growing up.

I didn't say anything. I just kept chewing and fantasizing. It was probably a pipe dream.

Another pipe dream. But I would look into it. I was interested. Probably nothing would come of it, but it would be something fun to research on the internet. I liked to dream about leaving the hotel someday, about doing something that was my own. I liked to think about that.

My social life kept finding new lows. A cocktail waitress at work played matchmaker, setting me up with an older friend of hers.

"She's mature, like you, but really cool."

"Really cool" lasted for two dates. Then we realized both of us were just making each other really depressed.

A young bar back I'd hired introduced me to his mother, who liked to come into Oliver's to see her son working. She was divorced, had a cute laugh, seemed fun-loving. We went out a couple of times, but besides hanging out in bars, I didn't know what else to do with her. And if I thought about us being intimate, the image of my bar back kept popping into my mind, smiling at me and asking if he should start calling me Dad.

Besides Leni, no one else I met had led to anything. Leni was the one woman who had connected with me in a meaningful way. She was someone I could imagine being with every day, to share the future with, maybe grow old with. But I had missed my chance with her by ending it so badly. I didn't have any expectations of achieving that with someone else anymore.

I didn't dwell on it all that much. I kept it tucked away, just trotted it out into my mind sometimes, mostly when I was alone, late at night, when my other responsibilities were unable to keep their grasp on me. When the morning came the dream was gone again. My mind settled in to the day before me. I went to work.

And I was at work when I found her again.

I was in the office looking through my email archives, trying to find a business contact. As I kept scrolling back, I thought I should delete a lot of old ones I didn't need anymore. That was how I found the email from Leni, back when we first met.

It was a Yahoo! address; all of our exchanges had been on AOL. I didn't even remember it. I opened it; she was just getting back to me about setting up a meeting place, the first one when we were at Greenlake.

I had deleted all her emails from my computer at home right after we broke up. I knew we wouldn't be in touch anymore. Keeping all the emails seemed like a hurtful reminder of how badly it had ended. How it ended because of me, because of how freaked out I got over 9/11.

That was eighteen months ago. I had put her out of my mind for the most part. I believed I had to; there couldn't be any going back. But I couldn't completely forget about her. There had been something very sweet and tender between us. She did everything she could to make me feel that I was special to her, that she appreciated me, that I was the one she had been hoping to come into her life. And she got sucker punched for it.

I hoped that she had rebounded from what I did to her, that she was happy, maybe with someone else, maybe not, but that she was strong, that I hadn't done any lasting damage to her.

I decided I had to write to her. She probably wouldn't get it anyway. She probably had dumped the Yahoo! account a long time ago, but I had to try, to at least make the effort. She had to know. It was my fault. I had blown it with her, and I shouldn't have. She was the best thing that had happened to me for years. She was a good woman, genuine, sincere. She asked for nothing except for me to love her back. That's all she needed from me, but I couldn't do it and pushed her away.

So, I told her. I wrote her all that, and I said I completely understood if I never heard back from her, that it was probably better for her if I didn't. I just hoped she was doing well. And I was sorry. And I was glad for the time we had together.

I clicked Send and the email disappeared. I thought that if I was lucky enough to hear back from her, if there was any opening for me to start over with her, I wouldn't mess it up again like I did the first time.

PART TWO

The Journey

After the Idea
February 2004–September 2004

CHAPTER SEVEN
February 2004

WHEN I RETURNED TO Seattle after attending Maggie's funeral, I had to repack for another trip I had scheduled, a business trip. I was being sent down to Las Vegas to check out what was being served in some of the finer hotels there, and to attend a food and beverage conference. My mission was to learn some new things for our hotel to share with the food and beverage manager, and maybe tweak the cocktail menu with a new item or two. In reality, they just wanted me to have a good time. It was kind of a bonus for being a good soldier for so many years.

I had been working there almost seventeen years, starting off as a banquet bartender and working my way up after a couple of years into being a full-time lead bartender in Oliver's. I'd done that for a decade, until I was tapped for an opportunity to move into management. After serving as restaurant manager for a year and then settling in as the bar manager, I rarely had to get behind the bar anymore. My job was to interview applicants, train employees, do the scheduling and the inventory, meet with the vendors, keep up standards. I was expected to keep the bar operating at a high level and to continue to bring new, innovative cocktails onto the menu. I was encouraged to seek out opportunities to learn new industry trends and practices.

My brother and the memory of Maggie were heavy on my mind, but I had to get back into my work and the tasks in front of me. I was in the basement office I shared with Steve Johansson, the food and beverage director. Because we both went by the same first name, we were usually differentiated by adding the first letter of our last name. He was Steve J, I was Steve B. Our office was our man cave, where we were surrounded by shelves of liquor, stacks of beer and wine cases, a cooler with beer kegs. The general manager, Paul Ishii, liked to come down and hang out with us when he wanted a break from all the women in the executive office. It was our sanctuary.

He was there talking to us as we sat around our desks. I was browsing through a trade magazine, which had a big section devoted to the conference I would be going to, the different vendors, the types of restaurants and bars that were going to be featured with representatives speaking about industry trends. I flipped through it, glancing absently while listening to Paul go on about how even the downtown rotary club was getting to be more women than men.

My eyes fell upon an advertisement. It was for a commercial cooking oven that I had never been aware of before. It was an electric-powered barbecue smoker that could be set to a temperature and for a designated time so as to allow the operator to leave it unattended. At the end of the cooking cycle, the meat would be fully prepared and ready to serve. It required no constant tending of the fire and the smoke, as did all the methods of making barbecue that I was ever familiar with in Texas. Even I could do it.

For the first time in a long while, and completely unexpectedly, a memory was awakened from deep within my mind.

My father's dream was to be his own boss. He was always thinking about and looking for some unique opportunity that would allow him to quit whatever job he was working and go into business for himself.

His first effort, going into the restaurant business with a drive-in bar and grill, ended disastrously. His concept included cute young women delivering trays to people's cars in the parking lot. He proved not to be a good manager of his product, his cash flow, or his employees, eventually running down to Mexico for a fling with one of his carhops, taking a couple of cases of beer and the weekend's receipts.

Being his own boss cost him his marriage. He lost his business, his home, and his family and went back to being a working stiff as a machinist in a metal-working shop. He didn't think he would ever try to start his own business again. It didn't stop him from dreaming about it, though.

"Whenever I pass through a town, or visit somebody in a place I'm not really familiar with, one of the first things I do is look around and see what kinds of businesses there are. I look and see what there is and then I ask myself: What's not here that people would want? That's always of interest to me. What kind of business isn't being offered here that people would really like to have?

On the rare occasions my father and I were together, usually trying to put down a case of Old Milwaukee— "best beer for the money," he liked to say—those are the kinds of wistful musings I'd have to listen to him impress upon me.

My heart was on being an actor in those days, something he could not fathom in the least. His only way to relate to me on any comparable level was to wax on his desire to run his own business. He saw me, though he couldn't comprehend what it was I was really doing, being similar, going my own way, not working for a paycheck and following some boss's orders. He wanted to see us both as yearning to be free and independent, our own men.

Ironically, years later, when he just about hit rock bottom, he got his wish.

When my mother suddenly died in a tragic accident, it ended my father's fleeting hopes that he might someday get back together with her. He wasn't sure what to do with himself, but he wanted to somehow get a fresh start. He relocated to Austin because my sister, Gerry, was working for a manufacturing company as a secretary, and she told him she could get him a job in their machine shop. He pulled his trailer into a mobile home park a couple of miles outside of town and not far from where the company's metal shop was. He was alone in the world and had a couple hundred dollars to his name.

The mobile home park was filled with Mexican immigrants and down-on-their-luck rednecks, people clinging to the fringes of life. They weren't even living paycheck-to-paycheck; their paychecks weren't able to bridge that gap. These folks were chronically behind the eight ball in life.

My father, despite his inability to accumulate wealth, was a proud and honest man. He paid his rent to the park's owner on time every month when he came through to collect. He listened to the old man complain about how he couldn't attract a better class of people, people like my father. He bemoaned how many empty spaces there were in the park and blamed it on the deadbeats who lived there; decent people wouldn't live around them. He railed at how difficult it was to pin down the other residents to get their rent money. He said he would be glad to sell the place someday and let somebody else deal with all the headaches of having to chase down the good-for-nothing trailer trash who dodged him day after day. A light bulb went on in my father's pea brain.

"Would you be inter'sted in leasin' the park to me?"

The old man sized him up. "You want to take on this riffraff?"

"I think I could handle them."

The two men agreed on a price both of them thought was fair. The old man chuckled that it would be worth letting my father have the opportunity because he wouldn't have to deal with the people anymore. He was sure my father was letting himself in for endless aggravation. My father didn't see it that way. The old man didn't live there. My father did, and he knew all those people. He watched them come and go. He knew where they worked and when they got paid. He drank beer with them on weekends around portable grills. He knew their children. He knew their pets. These people, especially the men, were not foreign to him. He had been a master sergeant in the army. He had no trouble looking these men in the eye and telling them exactly what he expected from them and exactly what would happen if he did not get it. He understood that all the park residents really needed was some applied discipline. Where the old man only saw problems, my father saw an opportunity.

Within six months the park was full. My father made sure the residents kept everything around their trailers clean and organized. He made rules that kept there from being any problems with the people living around one another. He had flexible, but reliable, methods of allowing them to keep their rent paid regularly. And he was there, on the property, every day.

The old man saw my father making his park a huge success. He offered to buy back the lease, but my father's price made him walk away cursing. He had secured a five-year lease with two renewable five-year options. Within a year, the park was making him more money than he had ever made working a job. He resigned from my sister's company and never worked for anyone else again.

After successfully operating his leased park south of Austin for a few years, my father bought three acres of land about ten miles away, east of Austin and close to the interstate highway. He was going to build his own park, but his wouldn't be intended strictly for mobile homes. He was interested in attracting RVs. These vacationers and snowbird retirees had the potential for better revenue by charging them daily rates instead of by the month. There was also less potential for problems because of a job being lost or a couple breaking up, or some other drama. They pulled in, stayed a day or two, maybe a week, then pulled out. Easy to do, easy to manage.

My father already knew exactly how he wanted to build the park, how many spaces, what materials for laying the pads, what facilities he would provide, where the septic tanks would be put in. He knew who he could contract to do the work and what part of the work he could do himself. And he knew that his was the first RV park going into that area. His closest competition was on the other side of Austin. The only other park in the area was the one he leased and managed farther south. He recognized a business that the area didn't have and that people coming through would want. Just like he used to tell me when we were drinking beer together.

By the time I was moving to Seattle to be with Kimberly, my father had two thriving locations. He could set his own schedule and didn't have to answer to anyone except himself for how he ran his business. He was his own boss. But cancer ended all that. After he passed away, I inherited money from an annuity my father had invested in when he became successful. We also took over owning his trailer park east of Austin. Tom, because he was a CPA, formed a corporation making himself president, with Gerry and me as officers. My brother and sister took responsibility for managing the park, including me in some of the decision-making, but mostly just providing me with an annual stipend from the profits. Just like when we were growing up, I, being the youngest, and now living the farthest away, wasn't much help.

After I saw the advertisement for the automated barbecue smokers, I initially put it out of my mind. The image of my father that flashed through me was only an instinctive reminiscence. He would have locked on to the advertisement with visions of its business possibilities. I was only associating it with my memory of him.

The ad caught my attention because I had grown up in Texas and barbecue had a storied tradition there. Grizzled pit masters were renowned and respected, their expertise gained through a lifetime of practice and dedication, built on the bedrock of cattle-raising generations before them. Barbecue was an art, a Zen-like adherence to technique and style. Barbecue was embedded in the lore and history of Texas, part of the essence of being a Texan. I had a visceral reaction to it, that was all.

But I had been away from Texas for decades. Barbecue wasn't something I gave any conscious thought to. I found the idea of the smokers interesting, though certainly not of any relevance to myself personally. But instead of tossing the magazine, like I usually would have after looking at it, I tucked it under a pile on the corner of my desk.

CHAPTER EIGHT

I ATTENDED THE CONFERENCE in Las Vegas and went through the motions of doing my work. I checked out bars and cocktails and menus, seeing if there were new and interesting ideas for me to export back to the hotel in Seattle. I sat in on seminars and presentations. I made some contacts, exchanged business cards, looked at some products.

But during the times I was alone, ambling through the Bellagio, my mind kept wandering, stewing about my life and the people in it. There was a restlessness about time passing and what I was doing with myself. Or perhaps not doing.

I kept thinking about my brother, about Maggie's children not having their mother anymore, my father's memory coming at me seemingly out of nowhere, and Leni.

She had responded to my Hail Mary pass email after considering it for a couple of days. Her reply to me indicated she was surprised to hear from me after so much time had gone by, but that she harbored no bad feelings toward me anymore. She was doing the same things, living alone; nothing had really changed for her.

That translated to me into the idea that the door was open enough for me to stick my foot in. That's all I needed. I spent months working my way back into her good graces, proving that she could trust me not to betray her again. And then I asked her to marry me and move into my house in Shoreline with me.

We were relative newlyweds, but neither of us was a spring chicken. Both of us were closing in on fifty years old. I wanted to feel like it was a new beginning for both of us.

I didn't want either of us to feel obligated to our past history. We had to accept each other's past, that we had children we cherished, ex-spouses to contend with, our extended families and friends, but I wanted to feel like we were making a new beginning together. We were going to write our own story, our new story, not just combine and incorporate each into a continuation of our past stories.

My problem, though, was that I didn't yet know what that story should be. We were doing what we had been doing. All those years of working at the Mayflower Park Hotel was by far, cosmically far, the longest I had ever worked one job. I was starting to reconcile myself that it might be where I would retire from. At my age, with my limited experience, where could I expect to go?

Leni was still a flight attendant. She wanted to reach the goal of ten years of service to earn lifetime flight benefits. After that, she imagined she would stay with the company as a gate agent or maybe in reservations, some kind of ground job to take her into retirement.

After we married, she moved into the house with me that I had been able to purchase three years earlier. So far, we were just continuing in the same way we had before we married. And now, roaming the casino in the Bellagio, I was haunted by thoughts of my father in the past, my brother in the present, and the life ahead in the future with Leni.

I didn't know what it all meant, but I felt like something was happening within me, something was building, or growing, or evolving. And then it appeared, like an aha! moment, like an epiphany.

An automated barbecue smoker.

I had thought of my father, who had been gone for over a decade. My father always wanted to have his own business, be his own boss. When it happened for him it turned out to be a business he was uniquely suited for. He was just at the point of reaching a comfortable retirement when cancer and emphysema snuffed out his life. He never really got to enjoy the success that had mostly eluded him his whole life.

My father was never pleased at my decision to go to New York when I got out of high school to pursue being an actor. It wasn't practical. It wasn't anything he could relate to or care about. I always felt there was a distance between us that could never be bridged.

My brother and I had a similar relationship. He was an accountant. His profession was all about business. Practical, rational, logical numbers. There was little common ground for us to share. We talked sports. I tried, pathetically, to play golf with him.

Leni and I were settling into a routine, not really seeing each other with inquisitive eyes anymore, starting to accept a presumed, daily continuance of who we had been before we married. We weren't doing anything new, anything that was uniquely our own story.

Suddenly, that all merged together in one connected vision tied together by an automated barbecue smoker. What would have made my father proud of me? Starting my own business.

How could I help my brother with his grief? Starting a business with him that we could plan and build together.

What could be the new path for Leni and me to embark on our own story? Starting a business, a business that could let us leave our jobs and work together on something.

The more I thought about it, the more perfect it was. My grandparents on my father's side had the most successful marriage I ever knew of in my family. They were together for sixty-two years. One passed away and the other followed in less than a year. They did everything together. They had a farm when their sons were growing up, and then they owned a general store for a few years. My grandmother developed a reputation for the tiered wedding cakes she produced in her kitchen, and my grandfather would be right there with her, cleaning up the frosting guns and baking pans as she went through them. They did laundry together, one rolling it through the wringer on the washtub, the other hanging it on the clothesline outside. I didn't see them that often because we didn't live close to their town, but I never saw one without the other until after my grandmother passed away.

I had not noticed any barbecue places in the north end of Seattle, where I had been residing for several years. I knew of some in other parts of town, the south end and over on the east side across Lake Washington. All those places were hugely popular. There was one, Pecos Pit, in the industrial district close to the baseball stadium that had been there for years. It was only open Monday through Friday for lunch, and they had lines every day. They didn't even open on the weekend. A rustic, hand- scrawled sign said "Open 11am to 3pm or when it's gone." The impression was that most days, by the look of the long line of people waiting to be served, it was the latter. I could virtually have the north end to myself until the competition caught on and tried to move in. I would have the whole market to establish and anybody else would have to catch up.

Again, I imagined my father assessing it with me: "What kind of business isn't being offered here that people would really like to have?" Now I was on fire. This was a whole new idea. A whole new paradigm. For the first time in a long, long time I had a conception of making my life truly meaningful again. I just had to completely reinvent myself and convince others I wasn't crazy.

I didn't have the first clue how to make barbecue. I didn't even know how to cut a brisket. I didn't know what ingredients went into making a decent barbecue sauce. In fact, I didn't know how to cook at all. I knew more about using a microwave than an oven. There were a lot of things I didn't know, but there were a couple of things I did. I knew I was from Texas, and it wasn't hard for me to slide right back into speaking like I did when I grew up. I had been working with food and beverage at the hotel for years. I knew about food cost and labor cost and front of the house and back of the house. I knew about budgets, profit and loss statements. I knew how to manage employees. And that was my plan. It wasn't that I needed to be that great at doing everything; I just needed to hire and manage employees who did. As long as I had the automated barbecue smoker that was dummy proof, I could learn everything else along the way. Most important, I knew I could win people over because I had been doing that as an actor, a bartender, a manager, and in my checkered history of transient jobs my whole adult life. If I was excited, I could get others to be excited with me. I knew I could do that. I was always good at "acting" like I knew what I was doing until I could catch up to somewhat actually *knowing* what I was doing.

I wasn't going to say anything to my wife yet. Or my brother. This was just a wild idea. It could pass. I could come to my senses and chalk it up to temporary insanity. I would read that advertisement again, maybe see if I could find a little information on the internet. I could look for some resources on how to make barbecue. And learning how to start a business. And maybe learning how to finance it. I was ready to go home and take another look at those smokers. I wanted to see if I could learn enough to start "acting" like I knew a thing or two.

CHAPTER NINE

WHEN I CAME BACK from Las Vegas, I filed my report to Steve J about a couple of cocktails and some hotel trends there that were gaining momentum and then quickly forgot everything about that trip except how it had ignited me to take action on my big idea.

I rummaged through the pile on my desk and found the magazine again. I took it home to look at the ad again more closely. Leni was away flying and I wouldn't have my kids until the weekend. I was alone in the house, with no distractions.

On the surface it all looked simple enough. You get some meat, you put some kind of seasoning on it, you put it in the smoker, you put some wood of some kind in the little tray in the bottom that was attached to an electric coil that ignited the wood during the cooking process, you shut the oven door, you set the push-button controls for a time of several hours and a low cooking temperature of your choosing, you push the final buttons, you stand back and admire your work, and then you walk away. The oven does the rest. No tending the fire and smoke, no prodding and poking or turning of the meat, no sitting close by or going outside to fuss with it. Just come back when it's done and take it out. It was perfect, the way you wanted it cooked every time. No problem. What was there to know?

The bottom of the ad listed a website for the company, Southern Pride. I liked the name. It sounded kind of redneck. Looking at their website, I saw several models of smokers, from small to giant. I focused on the small ones because they were the least expensive, about the same price as buying a late-model, used car.

The company was in Illinois. Huh, that was a bit of a surprise. I would have figured someplace more in the south. Maybe in Texas. But then, Kansas City was in Missouri. That town was supposed to have some pretty good barbecue. I had never been there. Maybe it was close to there.

It was a long way from where I was in Seattle. Then I remembered Leni had flight benefits. She and a spouse—that was me now—could fly domestically anywhere in the country that the airline flew into. There were other airlines that had reciprocal arrangements, so that for a nominal fee, we could go just about anywhere in the country. Anytime we wanted to. We just had to fly standby.

Leni could go on the company's website, where there was a dedicated employee section for travel. She could look at flight loads for trips throughout the company's system in any of the cities it flew into, seeing how available seating looked for days or weeks in advance. You could watch how a flight was booking right up to the time it took off, meaning you could make snap decisions about running out to the airport and jumping on a plane. She was constantly pushing me to take trips with her for a weekend, even just for a day, to fly down the coast to California or up to Canada.

Now I had a reason for using her flight benefits. A quick trip to Illinois. Just a little look-see, maybe a demonstration. I could ask some questions, hopefully nothing that revealed how clueless I was, get some ideas about how other restaurants around the country were using them, if they were becoming popular. Maybe I could meet a couple of restaurant owners they'd sold machines to.

It was too early to say anything to Leni about it. I would just file it away for now, come back to it later. The plan for better understanding the machine was hatched; now I needed to think about some other things.

Namely, how do you make barbecue? I knew it had to be cooked for a long time, many hours. I wasn't sure why. The meat needed to be seasoned, or brushed with sauce or something, before and during the time it cooked. It had to be cut up or carved or chopped or something when it was done. I really needed some kind of training, somebody who could show me how to do it, make it a system I could master and repeat, that I could train others to do.

Because that was what I wanted, to train others to do the cooking and serving. I wanted to be freed up to be the manager, the impresario. I wanted to be out front to greet and chat up the customers. To be able to do the marketing and brand building. To build up our reputation in the area and make the place popular and interesting, building a customer base. I wanted to make it so successful I would have to open a second place, and then a third. To have it be an idea that could become a franchise, maybe go nationwide. I would build an empire and expand the business into Texas, where I could have family members either work in the company or become franchise owners of their own.

The possibilities just went on and on.

ED MOLZAN PEERED WARILY and incredulously from behind his cramped desk through heavy, thick-lens glasses. He was a small man, a septuagenarian shrinking in stature as the years advanced. He took pride in wearing a suit and tie and coming in freshly shaved, his thinning hair combed back. He was a long-retired businessman who felt he could still offer some benefit from his lifetime of practical experience. He was a volunteer at the Small Business Administration in their mentoring program. As a member of the Service Corps of Retired Executives, he found it stimulating to listen to eager, aspiring young people sharing their hopes for starting a small business. However, today's consultation had him flabbergasted.

Ed was the first person I shared my unique and daring barbecue plan with. I found the SBA on the internet and wandered into their downtown office without an appointment. It just so happened that Ed had a cancellation, so I was able to go in and sit down with him for half an hour. I hadn't really planned on meeting with someone that day; I was just looking to get some information. But what the heck, what could it hurt?

"So, let me get this straight," Ed started, first rubbing his chin and then just staring off into space. "You want to open a barbecue restaurant."

"Yeah!"

"And you've never owned a restaurant before."

"No. But I've managed one for over a year at the Mayflower Park Hotel." I didn't mention that I hated the job. That I had asked Steve Johansson to hand it over to my assistant manager and let me go back to just running the bar.

"And you don't know how to make barbecue."

"Not yet. But I've been looking on the internet and I've found several possibilities for learning about it from very experienced people. I think if I can just get some good techniques for cooking the meat that I can train workers to repeat, the automated smokers will handle the rest."

"Well, yeah, it might be a good idea to learn to cook the food first. I mean, it's kind of important. Do you have a business plan?"

"A what?"

He sighed. "Have you thought about what your strategy is, your concept? A location? How many employees you want to have? Who the competition is? Marketing? A budget? Insurance? Starting capital? Do you have capital? Are you going to borrow it? From where, a bank? Lots of luck with that. A relative?" He shook his head. "You're going to need to slow way down. You have to learn how to walk before you try to run. In your case, you need to learn how to stand up before you even walk."

Ed had hit me in the face with some cold water.

"Huh. Yeah. Thanks, I guess I have a lot to think about."

"Look, I have some templates I can give you for writing a business plan. You should start there. I can give you some pamphlets about starting a restaurant business. If you're serious about this, do some homework, put some things on paper. Then come back and see me. Once you have a good plan, I can tell you some things you should do. But first, you need to put in some work. You need to understand what you're getting yourself into."

"OK, Ed. I get it. I'll make a plan." I looked him hard in the eye. "You'll see me again. I will be back."

"Fair enough. By the way, do you know how many restaurant startups fail and go out of business in less than three years?"

"I would guess quite a few."

"About half. In less than seven years, about eighty percent."

"Wow." This was sobering, but I didn't want to look weak. "Well, I'm not giving up."

"And you can bet, in every case, every single one of them thought they knew what they were doing." He sat back in his chair and gave me a wry smile.

Ed Molzan was right. I didn't know the first thing about what I was doing. I took the materials he gave me about writing a business plan for opening a restaurant and tried to use them, but it was difficult because there was so much I didn't know. I didn't know where my location would be or what I would have on the menu. I didn't know how many employees I would need. And I certainly didn't know how much it would cost and where I would get the money.

It was stupid. All I knew was that I saw this automated barbecue smoker and it had set me off. I felt like my reaction to that smoker was something connected to a part of myself that I had long ago left behind. I never would have dared to even try opening a barbecue place in Texas, but I could see myself making it work in Seattle, a place where a great many people weren't as familiar with it as they were in Texas. There wasn't a barbecue culture in the Northwest that was established for generations. I could do this if I just had confidence in preparing the food.

Years and years of hanging in there at the hotel made me feel like it had prepared me to take on this kind of business. I could work with employees, with vendors. I was comfortable with the kind of customer service that it would take to win people over. I knew I had something I could be uniquely suited for to make successful. I was the right person with the right experience in the right area of the country at the right time. But I was about ready to throw in the towel because it all just seemed too outrageous and impossible. And then I met John Head.

I found John on the internet. He called himself the director and chief instructor of The Culinary Institute of Smoke-Cooking. He administered their eight-lesson, home-study course in advanced grilling and wood-smoking barbecue techniques, the Master BBQ Cooking School.

We traded emails in which I peppered him with questions about how I could learn what I needed faster than taking an eight-lesson, home-study course. I just needed some good meat handling techniques that could let me throw the whole mess into my automated smokers and let them do their magic. And maybe he could show me how to cut a brisket.

His lengthy reply reiterated the value of their home-study course, but then included a passage that left me hearing triumphant harps and a swelling angelic chorus.

"However, if, as I read between the lines of your message, you are looking for true high-quality BBQ, why not stay with your own professional, organizational, and hospitality strengths and hire an expert pit master to set up the equipment, train the youngsters, and get you moving into a multi-restaurant situation?"

"It so happens that I would be available, on a short-term, contract basis, to do just that for you. I am going through a divorce and have been weighing my professional options. After years as a newspaper guy and a PR/media relations person, I am doing much more with BBQ these days and am looking for exactly the consulting type of situation you describe. Once I am done, your folks will have the expertise to carry on and expand as necessary."

Holy shit! A real BBQ expert, the director of the Culinary Institute of Smoke-Cooking himself, was available to work with me in starting my restaurant. He would even come to Seattle and do it.

I couldn't believe my luck. Was this perfect or what? It was a sign. I couldn't give up yet. There was still a lot that could go wrong, but I had to play this out. I had to see if John Head could teach me everything I needed to know to pull it off, to start my own restaurant.

The first thing was to write him back and propose that we meet face to face. I'd come out to Denver, where he was, and maybe we could try out a barbecue joint or two together. We could see if we liked each other, if we could work together. Neither of us had to feel obligated yet. We could just have a meeting, learn about each other. After that, we would take it from there.

Flying to Denver would require Leni's flight benefits. That would probably involve Leni wanting to know what I was using them for as well. The time had come for me to share my plan with my wife. Now she would find out just who the man she'd married really was.

CHAPTER TEN
March 2004

JOHN HEAD AGREED WHOLEHEARTEDLY to meet me in Denver, said he would be happy to show me some great barbecue out there. It looked like we wouldn't be able to do it for a few weeks yet, so I decided to hold off saying anything to Leni until I had a chance to think about things a little more. I wasn't sure how she was going to take it, so I wanted to feel like I had my ducks in a row when laying it all out to her.

Increasingly, the barbecue plan was more and more on my mind throughout the working day. My job didn't really entail giving much thought to it anyway. I mostly cruised around, schmoozing with workers, guests, the odd vendor who wandered in. I attended meetings, interviewed applicants, did inventory reports and financial projections. I had a cushy job and I knew it. I had to be crazy to think I would want to throw it aside to open my own barbecue restaurant. And yet I couldn't seem to get over it. I found that in all my conversations at work I had an antenna tuned for associations to my barbecue plan. I was talking to Jeff Thomas, a salesman from Bargreen Elling-son. His company had been supplying the hotel with all kinds of hospitality goods and equipment for many years. His boss, Jeff Gentling, had impressed heavily on him to treat the Mayflower Park Hotel account with sincere defer-ence. The older Jeff had babied the account for years with Mrs. Dempsey, earning her trust. He wanted his protege, the younger Jeff, to give complete satisfaction to anyone he worked with there. He and I were talking about supplies for the bar when Jeff mentioned that another restaurant they were helping to open was using the same glassware we were.

"You guys are helping somebody open a restaurant?"

"Sure. That's what we do. Design, construction, equipment installation, everything. From start to finish, whatever's needed."

"Do you help small-time operators, or just the big corporate guys?"

"Everybody. Anybody. Why, you want to open a restaurant?" He looked at me openly, curiously, ready for anything I might throw at him.

"Well, Jeff," I lowered my voice, "just between you and me…"

"Of course." He moved in conspiratorially closer. "There is this idea I've got for a restaurant…something I think I could be well suited for… something I think there might be a great market opportunity to establish in the north end."

"What? What?" He was all ears.

"A barbecue restaurant." I watched him closely for his reaction. He broke into a smile and considered it for a moment. "Ah, that's interesting. Yeah, you're right. I don't know of any out that way until you get up to Everett. You know how to make barbecue?"

"Well…" I shrugged. I didn't want to look like a complete fool. "I am from Texas, you know."

"Yeaaaahhh, there's good barbecue down there. You learned it down there?"

"I certainly learned how to eat it down there. But here's the thing, Jeff: I've got a lead on collaborating with someone on this project who is very experienced with barbecue, knows all the ropes. He is ready to consult with me. And my plan is to use something I came across recently, a fully automated barbecue smoker. It's from a company called Southern Pride."

"Oh yeah. They're great. We sell those."

"You sell Southern Pride smokers?"

"Sure, I know their Seattle rep. You want to meet him?"

What a quirk of fate. "I do. I do. But not yet. I'm trying to work out a business plan and some more details. I haven't really found a good location yet. I'll take you up on it later, though. Thanks."

"You want to talk to one of our restaurant designers? He could probably be really helpful in making a design plan. He could even scout some locations with you, help you find a good spot. I think he lives in the north end."

"How much does it cost to consult with him?"

"For you, no charge." I looked at him in disbelief.

"I'm joking, but seriously, he wouldn't charge you to have a meeting, draw up a plan of the equipment needs and a general floor plan. He gets paid when you actually have him do the design, the construction, and order the equipment. It's an investment for him."

"Well, sure, I'd love to give him a call. What's his name?

"Jeff Winter."

"Another Jeff? Of course. Is that like a requirement for working at Bargreen/Ellingson?"

"It doesn't hurt."

"HEY, HONEY, HOW WOULD you like to go out for dinner tonight?"

Leni stopped rummaging around in the refrigerator and turned to me brightly. "Really? You want to?"

We didn't go out to dinner all that often. Taking her out to dinner so she didn't have to cook was always a pleasant diversion from our routine.

"Where do you want to go?" she asked with a smile of anticipation.

"There's a little barbecue place I heard about out on the Bothell-to-Everett highway. I thought it might be fun to check it out."

"Barbecue?" Her smile faded. She looked at me quizzically. "So, you want to eat that, do you?" She nodded her head with some resignation. "Barbecue. OK."

One of the things I had been learning about my new wife was her eating habits. She was not adventurous in trying new or exotic cuisines. She had grown up on Vashon Island, the daughter of a commercial fisherman. Her Norwegian roots were in basic meat, fish, and vegetables. She was not one to stray far from what she was used to.

"Well, I have something I want to tell you about, an idea I had, and I thought going to this place might be a good way to do it."

"What do you mean? What kind of idea?"

"You'll see. I'll tell you all about it while we're having dinner."

"You'll have to do the ordering for me. I don't know what any of that stuff is. And I hope they don't goop too much of that sauce on it. It's so messy."

Leni was not completely inexperienced with barbecue. I had recently taken her with me to Texas in the summer after we got back together. It was a happy occasion as Tom's daughter, Amy, was getting married. It was also our last happy time with Tom and Maggie together, only weeks before she was diagnosed with cancer.

The reception was held outdoors on a ranch in the hill country. Barbecue was the theme for the meal. Leni mostly picked at her plate, but was gracious about not making any comments to anyone about it not being to her liking. She chatted a lot with Maggie because Tom and Maggie were the only ones familiar to her from when they had visited in Seattle. Maggie and Leni felt some kinship in both being second wives at the wedding, watching Tom's daughter from his first wife walking down the aisle. Maggie wasn't eating much from her plate either, complaining that her stomach had been bothering her; some kind of indigestion was plaguing her. She had been to the doctor, but he was still trying to help her figure it out. She said it was frustrating.

After that trip, the subject of barbecue had not come up between us again. Until now. The first of what became many barbecue joints I dragged Leni into was called Big Al's BBQ and was tucked into a nondescript strip mall on a state highway north of Seattle.

"How did you find this place?" Leni asked, while using her fingernail to scrape a small congealed glob from the red-and-white-checkered vinyl covering that draped our cafe table.

"One of the regulars at Oliver's told me about it. He lives up here in Mill Creek. He says it's pretty good."

"Well, it's not easy to notice it from the road."

"Yeah, people really like that about these kinds of places. They like finding them in out-of-the-way spots and then telling other people about it. It's like a secret, like only a few people know where a good barbecue place is, kind of a cult following."

She gazed up at the "menu," words crudely scrawled on a crookedly hanging chalkboard behind the service counter.

"Sounds like a hard way to stay in business."

The conversation wasn't moving in the direction I wanted it to, so I changed the subject.

"What do you feel like eating?"

"I don't know. I don't know what any of this stuff is. Whatever you want. Let's just share something. Do they have a salad?"

I went up to the counter, where a goth-looking young woman with a nose ring rang up my order of the large combination platter that would give us a good sampling of all their meats. While she was taking my side choices, I noticed an automated smoker in the kitchen area, but it didn't look like the same one I'd seen advertised. It looked older, more worn, slightly smaller.

"Is Big Al here? I'd like to ask him about his smoker."

"There is no Big Al."

"What? But...the name of the place..."

"He sold the place to John. John's not here right now," Nose Ring said.

"How long's John had the place?"

"Oh, a couple of months or so. Not too long."

"How's it goin'? You guys doin' pretty good here?"

She gave me a blank stare. "All right, I guess. I haven't been here very long. It's busier on the weekends."

We got our plate and Leni mostly watched me devour it. She had small tastes of everything, agreeing with me that it was all fine for the most part.

"It's not really my kind of thing," she said, "but if you're happy, I'm happy. I know you used to eat this kind of food when you lived in Texas. You don't find it so much up here, do you?"

"Well, that's kind of what I wanted to talk to you about."

She looked at me with curiosity. "You wanted to talk to me about... barbecue?"

I talked in low tones. There were only a couple of other people in the place, but I didn't want to draw attention to us.

"Look, I know this place isn't really the best example. I mean, it's OK, but...remember when we first got married and we talked about how it would be nice to do something different from what we've had to do for so many years? Something that was really our own, that was going in a whole new direction?"

Her curiosity was shifting into something a little more uneasy. She started glancing around and then looked at me with some concern.

"Uh-huh, and this place has something to do with that?"

"How many barbecue places have you noticed where we live in Shoreline?"

She shook her head as she pondered the question.

"There are none! At least none that I'm aware of right now. And the reason is barbecue is finicky food to have to make. It takes a long time to cook, hours and hours, and it has to be tended to and watched over. But I've come across some new technology that has been applied to the making of barbecue. The guy here is using it. Not the same kind I'm looking at, but something just like it. If this automated smoker oven I'm looking at really works, it could be a game-changer. Lots more people will be looking at getting into the barbecue business and the public—paying customers—will have a lot more of it around them to take notice of."

She looked at me like she was ready to get a word in edgewise, but I was on a roll.

"This is the kind of business I could do. I can use my Texan background to give an authentic image to being the face of a BBQ place. If we can get it up and going before other people figure out that there is a wide-open market in the north end that has no barbecue places for thousands and thousands of potential customers, well, it could be a great opportunity.

And it could be ours, our own business. Something that could let me finally leave the hotel, that could let you leave flying. We could do it together."

Now I paused so she could say something. She said nothing for several seconds. She might have been trying to decide if I was playing some elaborate practical joke on her. Finally, she said, "You want to open a restaurant?"

"A barbecue restaurant," I said pointedly. "It's providing a service in an area where there's an unmet need. And there's new technology that's making it much more accessible for it to be mastered. And I'm exactly the right kind of guy to be doing it. There's something there."

She looked like she didn't want to hurt my feelings or be a killjoy to my unbounded optimism, but it was hard for her to jump on board with me.

"Sweetheart, I don't know anything about working in restaurants. I've never done that."

"You know customer service. You know how to work with people. You serve people all the time. What I'm talking about is doing it in a way where you don't have to take off and land between serving them. I'm talking about finding a way for you to make a plan not to have to fly anymore."

That seemed to be winning her over more.

"It would be nice not to have to fly, not do the overnights, sleep in those hotel beds. Now that we're married I just get so lonely out there. I just want to be home. I want to be with you."

"Well, I would like to do something different, too. Finally break away from the hotel. I don't know how either of us could do it unless we did something completely new. Unless we really took a risk."

"Starting a restaurant would certainly be that. Doesn't it cost a lot of money to start a business like that?"

"Yeah, that's a part I haven't completely worked out yet. We would need to put out some money for it. I'm not sure how much, but probably at least a hundred thousand or so. Maybe more. Maybe a lot more."

"And that's the thing: We don't have that kind of money available to us. Do we?"

"No. Not right now. You're right, it's crazy, just a stupid idea. I got carried away because there was so much about it as a business that seemed right. It seemed perfect for me to be the guy to do it. I don't know how we would make it happen, though."

"I'm sorry. I don't mean to be negative. It's really nice to see you so excited about something. But...barbecue? Really?" She had to laugh.

"I know. It is...a unique idea. But you know what, I'm going to keep looking at it. It probably won't come to anything, but I want to keep exploring. If nothing else, I'll have some fun with it. I've come across a couple of people I've already learned a few things from. I just want to go a little further before I completely give up on it. Is that all right with you?"

She gave me a warm smile. "Sure, that's all right with me."

"Just do me a favor. Don't mention anything to anybody else about it. Your friends or your family. Or my family; especially not my family. Later on, if anything comes from it, I'll bring it up when I'm ready. I wanted to tell you, but I don't really want anybody else to know right now. Not yet."

"My lips are sealed." She cast a wary glance around the room one more time and chuckled. "No one would believe me anyway."

CHAPTER ELEVEN

JEFF WINTER DIDN'T ASK me where I was going to get the money. He didn't ask me if I knew how to make barbecue. He didn't give me any bemused smirks or raised eyebrows of bewilderment. He simply treated me professionally as a prospective client. And on the day I met him, he saved me from completely giving up.

When Jeff greeted me at the reception desk on the sales floor of Bargreen Ellingson and ushered me into his cubicle of an office, he exuded a calm and unassuming confidence. He was in his mid- thirties, of medium height and build, with the beginnings of a potbelly creeping over his waistline. He was shaved bald with stubble that showed around his domed head. He was serious in his manner, but friendly and open to easy conversation. He was younger than me and assumed I was an accomplished hospitality professional from one of their preferred and long-standing accounts who must have a deep understanding of the food and beverage industry. I wasn't about to set him straight.

After we traded some pleasantries about where we worked, he asked me what I had in mind to do, when I wanted to do it, and how I thought he could help me with it. Between studying the template of a business plan Ed Molzan had given me and the layout of the strip mall location of Big Al's BBQ, I could at least give him a reasonable answer to those questions.

"Well, of course it sounds like you have given a lot of thought to your concept and you have solid ideas about the area you want to locate in."

"Of course," I deadpanned. We nodded at each other.

"And the budget you have in mind?"

"Bingo. That's where I could use your help. I need to do a little more research on barbecue places I can find in the area to nail down more specifically the kinds of equipment I'll need."

"Yeah, we can get pricing for anything you think you want. Would you buy an existing restaurant or build out a raw space? An existing restaurant could have a lot of the elements you would need already, so you would only have to adapt it to your concept. A raw space costs more to build out, but you can make it exactly the way you want it, and you start with everything new. Or you might buy some used equipment, if you can find it. We have some in our warehouse from remodels and upgrades we've done, or there are some other stores that deal in used equipment down First Avenue south of the stadiums."

"Definitely. I hadn't really thought about places like that. I'll take a look."

"It sounds like you have a flexible timeline for wanting to open. That's fine. You should take your time and find the right location. It's not uncommon for ideas like this to take several months or more. We'll be here. We'll be ready when you are. If you want me to look at some locations with you, I can meet you there to make an assessment."

"Really? You would come look at a place with me?"

"Sure, if it'll help. It just has to be toward the end of the workday so that I don't have to come back downtown. You're looking at locating in the north end and I live out that way. It's not out of my way to meet you up there."

Now I was ready to look for my location.

ED MOLZAN COULDN'T STOP grinning at me. He listened to me expound on my company description, my products and services, my marketing plan, my operational plan, and my management and organizational team. I told him about Big Al's BBQ and a couple of other places I'd checked out in the south end. I told him about my general contractor and consultant, Jeff Winter, and how we had already scouted three location possibilities in the area I was interested in. I told him my wife and I were planning a weekend business trip to Denver to meet with my culinary consultant, John Head. All of the pieces were coming together nicely.

Ed pushed back in his chair, raised his chin, and squinted at me through the bottoms of his thick, dark-framed bifocals. "So, you've been doing your homework. You think you know what you're getting yourself into? You still want to do this?"

"I think I'm ready to take the next step, Ed. That's why I'm back here today."

"And what do you think the next step is?"

"I need to figure out the money. I want to see if I can get a loan. How do I go about getting a loan from the SBA?"

"The SBA doesn't make loans. It refers qualified small businesses to banks who have agreed to underwrite SBA loans. You have to go make your case to one of them."

"Do you have a list of them in the area you can give me?"

"I do, but just hold on there. Not so fast, not so fast."

He leaned forward on his desk and clasped his hands together. He took a moment to think and then looked me in the eye.

"You've got a lot of ideas worked out about what you want to do and the steps you want to take, but where are the numbers? How much do you have to invest? Are there other investors? Who are they and how much are they putting in? How much do you want to borrow? What are you using for collateral? What are your cost projections, startup expenses, your sales forecast? How long will it take you to get to break even?

I put up my hands. "I got your point. I plan to have my brother help me with all that. He's a CPA."

"Your brother? You haven't mentioned him. Is he going to invest?"

I paused.

"Is that a no?"

"I'm not sure yet. But he'll be working closely with me."

"Where is he? Why isn't he here with you?"

"He's in Texas."

"Texas! Well, why don't you go down there to start your barbecue restaurant? Isn't that what everybody eats down there?"

"I'm here. I want to start it here. If it works out, then later on we might look at starting one down there."

"Does he like that idea? What does he think about your plan so far?"

"He doesn't know yet. I haven't told him about it. I wanted to wait until I had more of the details worked out before I brought him on with me."

Ed just nodded his head at me with that shit-eating grin.

"Let me get you that list of banks. Go run your ideas by a few of them. See what kind of feedback they give you. It'll be a good way of knowing where your weaknesses are. Then come and tell me what they say. I'm interested to hear what they think of your barbecue restaurant plan. That should be a pretty good story."

Ed had a knack for bringing me back to reality.

I did my homework. Taking Ed's templates, I started developing the beginning of a business plan. I created an executive board with myself and Leni as president and vice-president, managing daily operations. Tom was secretary, overseeing all accounting and control procedures. I envisioned an operation that provided high-quality smoked meats with accompanying delicious side dishes and desserts that were attractive, comfortable, and inviting. I mapped out options for catering, for pickup or delivery for large group orders.

I constructed a menu based on what I was seeing being offered by all the barbecue places I could find in the Seattle area. I noted all relevant competition anywhere close to the north end and how we could be distinctive from them to attract customers. I plotted out a strategy for how large an operation we would have, how many employees, how many customers we could seat, what average check price we were looking for.

I utilized my experience as a bartender and manager to include plans for a full bar and the amount of revenue I projected for it to produce. Jeff Winter helped me to build an estimate of equipment costs, construction or renovation costs, license fees, the inventory and supply expenses for startup.

I tried to account for every contingency, to anticipate any questions about what I was doing, how I was going to do it, and why it would succeed. And then I started going into banks. I walked into at least half a dozen, asking to speak to a loan officer.

I was always treated politely and listened to attentively while I enthusiastically described what was my surefire opportunity to capitalize on there being no barbecue places anywhere in the north end of Seattle. I was asked pertinent questions about my experience and background, and even encouraged a time or two. But then I would always be handed loan applications. That was where the rubber met the road. They wanted to know what my assets and liabilities were. They wanted three years of tax returns. They wanted to know how much of my own money was going into the business and where it was coming from. If anyone else was starting the business with me, they wanted to know all the same information from and about them.

Thank you for coming in. Good luck.

I was realizing that no bank was going to touch this. If it was going to happen, it would have to be my own money. Or, possibly, family money, like my brother and sister. I didn't like the idea of that. I didn't imagine they would either.

I repeatedly came up against a brick wall, an obvious and seemingly insurmountable obstacle to going any further with this hare-brained idea of trying to do something I had not one inkling how to do. I would be ready to let it go, not waste any more time or effort with a pie-in-the-sky pipe dream.

And then the next step would present itself.

I was at the end of the bar during happy hour, checking in with the staff and chatting up the regulars like I always did. At the other end was Rocky, a swarthy, mafioso-looking guy with slicked-back dark hair. He was in his business suit and a cashmere overcoat, expounding for the bartender and anyone else close by who was interested in listening.

What caught my attention was when he mentioned he had a friend he was trying to help sell his restaurant in the north end. I worked my way over to where he was at the end of the bar so we could talk quietly together.

"Say, Rocky, this friend of yours trying to sell the restaurant, where is it?"

"You interested?"

"I could be. I have an idea I'm working on, something that's not in the north end. I'm looking for a place that could work for it."

"What kind of restaurant?"

I looked around because I didn't want others listening in. Rocky picked up on that and understood, so he leaned in closer to me.

"I'm thinking about a barbecue restaurant. Nobody's doing that in the north end."

He smiled at me. "Huh, barbecue—yeah, I see. That's interesting. Yeah, that could work with this place. It's in Mountlake Terrace. It's Italian. Pete owns it—I've known him for years. He's been there forever. But he's gettin' old—he'd like to retire. He's having some health issues, ya know? He would probably make you a pretty good deal."

"How big is the place?"

"Oh, I don't know, maybe fifteen, twenty tables in the front. But it's the back where he makes his money. That's where the bar is. The bar has a lot of regulars been comin' there for years."

"Oh yeah, a good bar business?"

"Sure, that would be right up your alley. You know how to make barbecue?"

"I gotta guy, he's an expert."

"Ohhh, that's good. Yeah, you should go talk to Pete. He's there every day, slingin' the pasta and flippin' pizzas in the kitchen. Tell him I sent ya."

"Thanks, Rocky, I'll look him up. I'll let you know what I find out."

"Yeah, yeah, you do that. And you let me know if you need anything. Anything at all. You let me know. I'll take care of ya."

Rocky didn't seem the sort of guy I wanted to be indebted to.

CHAPTER TWELVE
April 2004

IT WAS TIME TO go see my expert. John Head and I had exchanged several emails and agreed on a Saturday for Leni and me to come meet him in Denver. Leni had arranged for our flight through her benefits. We'd fly in, John would pick us up, we'd try some Denver barbecue places and talk shop, and then he would take us back to the airport for our return to Seattle that evening. In and out, easy-peasy.

John was there, exactly as he had said he would be. To me, that was a great beginning. It showed he was a man who could be counted on. He was a little older than me, maybe close to my brother's age. He was rotund, about medium height, and had a beard and perimeter-domed hair. He made me think of Burl Ives or a man who could seasonally moonlight as a shopping mall Santa Claus. He was jovial, easy to talk with, comfortable to be with. I felt the man I had traded emails with was who I hoped he would be, and I tried hard to make him feel the same way about me.

We drove into Denver and had lunch at a place called Caldonia's. John presided, selecting what we ate, and we talked about the cooking techniques used in various places around town. He pointed out nuances about the ribs we were scarfing and the barbecue sauces we were trying. But mostly, he was looking for every opportunity to inspire us with trying out his home-study course, the Master BBQ Cooking School.

He was talking a mile a minute and I was more focused on the ribs I was slavering over, but I understood something about the school being presided over by his ex-mother-in-law, who apparently took over from her deceased husband, who it seemed had started the whole ball rolling. Even though John and his wife had parted ways less than amicably, he wasn't ready to forego staying deeply involved with her mother's business. She was getting well on in years, and John saw himself as the heir apparent in carrying on the Culinary Institute of Smoke-Cooking into the foreseeable future. Sounded reasonable to me.

"Look, John, your home-study course sounds great, but I plan to let my automated barbecue smoker do all the work. I don't really have time to learn all the ins and outs of smoking meat. What I would like is just a solid method for cooking our meats that we can replicate every day, something that we can easily train new people to do when we need to. And I'd really like you to be the guy to come out to Seattle and do that with the first crew I hire. And I'll fly you to Seattle and pay you to do it."

He was flattered. "Well, you know, since I've gone through this somewhat unpleasant separation from my wife and I'm having to get used to living on my own, I've started thinking I might like to do some traveling to see if I can help people, such as yourselves, get your places started, and also promote CISC in different parts of the country."

CISC. It took me a second to understand he meant his home-study course. He continued, "I enjoy driving. I wouldn't mind making a trip out there and spending a few days with you."

"Really? And then drive back? From Denver to Seattle?"

"It's relaxing. I like seeing the country, stopping along the way if I choose."

We continued our tour, stopping at a place called Brothers BBQ, started by a couple of guys from England who reputedly had toured around America trying barbecue joints. We looked at a place called Sam Taylor's, run by a black pit master in the southern tradition, who also offered fried catfish and collard greens. Everywhere we went, I picked up menus to take home and refer to.

He regaled us continuously along the way with stories about barbecue, about Denver, and about different people he had taught, coached, or consulted for over the years. Between John and me, Leni had hardly gotten a word in edgewise, but she seemed content with being part of the adventure. She wasn't quite sure what to make of it all. It was certainly an interesting way to spend a Saturday.

When we got to the airport and it was time to say our goodbyes, John offered up a proposal.

"How about I come out over the Fourth of July and stay a few days? We can hunt out possible locations if you haven't decided on one yet. I can bring a little water-smoker I have that has been sitting around for a long time. We can play with cooking some meats, some seasoning techniques, then I'll leave it all with you to practice with when I go home."

"That would be wonderful. And we'll make sure you have a good time seeing Seattle."

"Well, that sounds like we both win."

When Leni and I came back from Denver and meeting John Head, I was inspired that we could really do this. John made me feel like he was completely on my side. He genuinely wanted to teach me and help me, not so much for making money, but because he loved the feeling of teaching someone like me about something that was so important to him. He loved barbecue. He was passionate about it. I didn't know how I could make it work financially. I didn't know if I could find a location that would work. But I felt that, with John on my side and with him coming to Seattle to help me, I could legitimately develop a professional approach to the food I would be selling. And I felt with Jeff Winter helping me, I had someone who could have my location fully equipped and ready to go, when and if I could just locate it. Ed Molzan was my go-to guy for checking in with progress reports, next-step advice, and generally keeping me on track for moving forward. Leni was solidly behind me, albeit not particularly as invested in the idea as I was. She was nonetheless willing to help me to whatever extent I called upon her to.

I knew who the next person to approach with my barbecue plan was. I was at the stage where I needed his input, his expertise, his collaboration. I needed his approval, his validation. And I was very nervous about whether I could receive any of those things from him. He was my brother. Tom and I had never worked closely with each other on anything. We rarely even hung out together without other family members with us. If we were alone and forced to have an extended conversation, we couldn't last ten minutes before awkward silences hung in the air between us.

The only business conversations we ever had were about our father's RV park. Tom, Gerry, and I had inherited it over a decade earlier. We weren't sure in the beginning how long we would keep it, but Tom and Gerry did such a great job of maintaining and managing it, the RV park had become a steady source of supplemental income for the three of us. We always worked cooperatively on any decisions to be made. The RV park served as a common bond for us, something we shared and cared about. Something we took pride in because it had been our father's. I felt he would have been very proud of how we'd carried on with it. And Tom was central to that. He was the president of our corporation. He was the architect of our business strategy with it. He was the strongest voice, the one Gerry and I looked to for leadership.

But the RV park was something between the three of us, something to which my sister was an equal contributor. I knew I wanted to include her in my barbecue plan. I wanted her to be involved in some way. She was very good in the kitchen and I felt she could work closely with me when I was fine-tuning some of the side dishes we would offer. She could help me with giving some southwestern authenticity to the menu. However, my brother had been my inspiration. He had been the one whose misfortune had planted the seed in me. But it was more than that. Gerry and I were always close. We talked, shared our feelings, stayed involved with each other. Tom and I had never been able to do that. I saw the barbecue idea as a bridge, as the vehicle that could help us find a common interest and enthusiasm.

Only I was afraid that he wouldn't see it the same way, that he wouldn't take it seriously. In fact, that he would scoff at me. I was afraid that when I shared my barbecue plan he would dismiss it as me being impulsive and impractical again. Like when I went to New York to be an actor. Just off in a fairyland again. Something I would be excited about for a while and then move on when I realized I couldn't really do it. And he was right. If he shot me down or if he even just didn't have an opinion one way or the other, I would crumble. My whole half-baked, crazy, ridiculous, cockeyed sham would come crashing down. So, this was a conversation I was very nervous about having. I was going to have it. And it would be soon; it would have to be. But I would want to feel ready, able to give lots of information about all I had done and learned about it. Answer any and all questions he might ask. I wanted to feel like I had all my ammunition, that I was as ready as I could be. It would have to be soon. Very soon.

I continued to go to work every day like normal. I didn't feel safe sharing my scheme with anyone there yet. I was afraid it might not be taken well, that I was making plans to leave. Of course, it wasn't really any kind of plan, just a fantasy, albeit a more developed fantasy than the way it began. The truth was, I very much appreciated my job. I was given great support, had numerous friendly relationships with coworkers, vendors, and customers. I made a good living. In fact, it was the only job I ever had in my life from which I could even claim with a straight face to have made any kind of living. I knew I was extremely fortunate to have that job and I was grateful for it.

Yet this desire in me to do something on my own had become deep and powerful. I thought about it constantly. Was it my midlife crisis? I was going to turn fifty that year. For most men, more successful and already established in their careers, it might be a fancy car or a boat, taking up skydiving or mountain climbing. They might succumb to leaving their marriage of many years or having an affair with a younger woman. Men do stupid things, and after turning fifty, their stupidity gets more creative and more ambitious.

The haunting contagion of a midlife crisis is rooted in fear. Fear of life slipping away, opportunities lost, dreams permanently deferred. Fear that the man you were, or thought you were, is no longer and will never again be. Fear of the end. The inevitable end.

Do I have anything left, any gas in the tank? Can I take one more swing at life, make one more attempt at scaling a summit? It's now or never. It's almost, but not quite, too late.

These are the obsessing, lingering, unconscious urges lurking within a man facing midlife. Was that what was motivating me? Quite possibly. And that was why I was being very careful about keeping my idea to myself and only sharing it very selectively. I might come to my senses. I might yet have common sense prevail. It would be a sad and disappointing acceptance. A resignation that there wasn't to be any more for me. That I was already as much as I would ever be. But, at least, I wouldn't make a complete public fool of myself.

Over the weeks and months, I had been chasing the intoxicating lure of an automated barbecue smoker, and I was brought back from the brink of abandoning the whole potential fiasco by a series of serendipitous encounters that followed upon one another like a trail of breadcrumbs. Ed Molzan, John Head, Jeff Thomas, Jeff Winter, Rocky. Each of them appeared when they were needed to keep me intrigued so I would take just one more step, look at it just one more time. Was there a higher power watching, willing to grant me as much slack in the rope as I needed at exactly the time I needed it? Was that higher power giving me enough slack to pull myself up to my dream or enough to finally hang myself when it all came crashing down?

Before I could muster up the courage to talk to my brother, before I could seek his crucial help and support in going forward, I wanted to feel like my higher power was still guiding and helping me.

And then I ran into Bob Littell.

I'd met Bob years before, in the early '90s, when I was referred to him by Kimberly's real estate agent sister, Lynne. He was an independent—and

I mean completely independent—insurance salesman and financial adviser working by himself downtown out of a small office around the corner from the Mayflower Park Hotel.

I was a husband and father at the time and I'd started thinking about establishing some kind of financial security. Bob sold me the first life insurance policy I ever had. He steered me into my first mutual fund, which I made small, automatic monthly contributions to and which eventually helped me purchase the house Leni and I were living in. He prompted me to buy Starbucks the first time they publicly offered stock. Bob had helped me make some good investment choices and I trusted him.

Bob was an affable guy, fun and always happy to see me. I met him one day on the sidewalk coming out of a bank with some application papers in my hand after yet another fruitless pitch to a loan officer.

"How are you? How's the hotel? Whatta you up to these days?"

Bob, a big teddy bear of a man, was giving me his easy smile with that twinkle in his eye that showed he was genuinely interested in what I had to say. In that instant I made a snap decision. I poured out to him that I was working on a restaurant idea, something unique, and I was frustrated by talking to banks on the SBA list who didn't really seem interested in underwriting a loan for me. I thought all I had to do was show them a good idea for a small business and they could connect me to some government money to launch it. I was going nowhere and it was sapping me of my enthusiasm to persist with it.

Bob looked thoughtful. "What kind of restaurant?"

There it was. I was starting to feel some empathy for gay men who were afraid to come out of the closet.

"Bob, can you keep this between us? I mean, we don't really talk to any of the same people, but I don't want this getting around until I'm ready for that. Can you keep a secret?"

He almost looked hurt. "Sure, sure. I understand. Of course."

I gave him the whole song and dance. Nobody's doing it in the north end. Great opportunity to establish a new thing there. A trend getting super popular in the Seattle area.

"Barbecue, huh, yeah." He scrunched his face at me. "You know how to make barbecue?"

Oh, geez.

"I'm bringing in a pit master I know from Denver. He's going to help me set it up."

"Wow. That's serious. It sounds like you've really planned it out."

"Yeah. Well, there's some details to work out, but like I said, I'm having a hard time getting past square one, so I don't know if I can pull it off or not."

"Hmm, you know, I know a guy who's writing business loans at a small community bank over at the corner of Fifth and Virginia. He's really hungry to do some business. I bet he would be a good guy for you to talk to."

"Do they work with the SBA?"

"I don't know. But he's a good guy. If anybody would listen to you and really want to find a way to help, he definitely would. You should give him a try. Tell him I sent you. He knows me. Tell him I recommend you. For all the good that'll do you."

Bob had been downtown for years. He knew lots of people. A recommendation from him was not a bad thing.

"His name is Daniel Petzoldt. Give him a call."

The next day I walked into Sound Community Bank, which I had never heard of. They were not an SBA bank, but Daniel was happy to talk to me anyway. If I was recommended by Bob Littell, he definitely was interested to hear about what I was trying to do.

I had enough practice making my pitch to loan officers that it was easy for me to sail through the high points. I had a pit master (John Head), I had a project manager (Jeff Winter), I had a location I was seriously considering (Pete's Mountlake Terrace Italian restaurant, which I hadn't even gotten around to seeing yet), and I had a CPA to do all my accounting and financial statements (my brother, whom I had not spoken to yet). All the boxes were checked except for this one additional detail about funding.

Daniel was clearly juiced. His wheels were turning, and for the first time I had a loan officer who was taking me seriously.

"All right. Let's see what we have to work with here. I think we might be able to find a way to get you up and running."

What I had not learned from Bob, and would not know until way down the road later, was that Daniel Petzoldt had not yet ever written a business loan. He was brand new to the job, fresh out of training. I was, potentially, his first client. He wanted me as badly as I wanted him.

The one thing he seized upon was that I owned a home and was relatively debt-free. He concocted a plan that if I established a checking and savings account with their bank, and then refinanced my mortgage with their bank, he could leverage the equity to set up a line of credit. In addition, if my equity position in my house was strong enough, they could set me up with a business loan to boot. Daniel was gleefully positioning me to bet my house on my faith in an automated barbecue smoker. A machine I had only seen a picture of in a magazine and didn't know the first thing about.

I felt like I had hit a home run and was watching the ball sail over the fence.

CHAPTER THIRTEEN
May 2004

I LEFT TEXAS WHEN I was nineteen years old to go to New York City to be an actor. For my entire adult life I'd lived far away from any of my family. I saw them occasionally, when I ventured back for visits. There were a handful of times family members had traveled to where I was. But mostly, we stayed connected with sporadic phone calls or, more often in recent years, by email, and with some scribbled-on Christmas and birthday cards. We were close, yet at a distance. Familiar, but usually not in each other's lives.

The anchor that kept me moored to my Texas origins was my sister, Gerry. She was five years my senior. Tom was almost a year and a half older than her. Gerry spent the most time with me when I was a toddler and a small child, keeping me from harm's way, playing with me. She stayed the most involved with me when I was a teenager. She was the most persistent about visiting me in New York the first years I was there. My brother came once, but it was my sister with whom I had many more experiences out on the town. In the years after my mother died it was my sister who made sure I was kept in touch with, made aware of family gatherings, invited for vacations and holidays.

When I went to Texas it was always her home that was my initial destination. From there I would go see my father. From there it would be decided if my brother made the trip from San Antonio to come see me or if I would go down his way. I don't remember ever spending the night in my brother's home as an adult, either during his first marriage or his second one to Maggie. I always stayed with Gerry.

It wasn't that I didn't want to stay with Tom or that he didn't want me to. It just made more sense to stay with Gerry. We had always been close. It was natural for us to hang out together. Tom and I just had much less history together. And we had pursued very different paths in life. We didn't have much in common.

In recent years there was a new dynamic for me that made staying connected with the Texas family more meaningful. It was my children. I had failed both my daughter and then my son by not staying with their mothers. I forced them both to grow up with me being only a part-time dad. They didn't even get to share the same household growing up, mostly seeing each other when both were with me at the same time.

I always swore I didn't want to end up being my father and yet in some ways I'd surpassed him. At least he managed to give his children the same mother to grow up with.

It was important for me to expose my children to their Texas family every opportunity I got. I knew in all likelihood they would grow up living far away from Texas and never have much reason to stay connected with anyone down there. I at least wanted them to have a sense that there was family in the world they were part of, if even distantly.

In the '80s Gerry and her husband, Mike, purchased a time-share vacation condo on South Padre Island, close to the Mexican border at Brownsville. They took their children there every summer. Tom followed by getting his own unit in the same building a couple of years later. After that there was an opportunity every summer throughout the '90s and into the '00s for all of us to come together for some beach time and a day trip across the border into Matamoros. I took my children down there whenever I could. My hope was that they would internalize being part of the family. That someday, when I was no longer around, they would feel there was part of me that lived on for them through an extended family they were still a part of. It was a thin tether, but something I really wanted to at least try for.

Now it was the irrational mania over an automated barbecue smoker that was fueling my intense desire for a stronger family connection. I wanted to create a business my family could readily understand and relate to. They knew barbecue. At least, Texas-style barbecue.

My sister and I were very close. She would certainly be less intimidating to talk to first, less likely to shoot me down. But it wasn't her I really needed at this point. The key would be convincing my brother to help me. It had to start there. And because there was no precedent to the call I was going to make, no time I had ever reached out to him like this before, it was the scariest thing I had ever done with someone in my family since I told my mother over thirty years earlier that I wanted to move to New York and be an actor. I couldn't put it off any longer. I picked up the phone and made the call.

"Hello?" I heard my brother's voice as he immediately answered.

He picked up the phone right away. It didn't go into voice mail. Maybe that was a good sign. Of course, he'd been using a cell phone for some time, longer than I had, so I guess answering his phone on the first ring wasn't all that uncommon.

"Oh, what a surprise," he said when he heard my voice. "How have you been?"

That was good. Good. We could lob a few softballs. Make some small talk.

"Oh, I guess I'm still adjusting," he said after we talked a while. "It's been pretty tough to get used to. Becky and Steve have been very sweet. They always check in with me. So do Maggie's sisters."

He thought it was yet another condolence call. Becky and Steve were Maggie's children from before they were married. He wasn't going to see it coming. I thought that maybe I should wait.

He went on, "I just try to stay busy, try to keep my mind occupied and not sit around feeling sorry for myself. How about you? Anything new?"

I decided it was now or never. I wouldn't have the guts to make the call again. I talked for the next ten minutes without stopping, it felt like almost without taking a breath. I told him everything, but this time I didn't embellish, I didn't try to make him believe anything that I only hoped could be true. He didn't need to ask if I knew how to make barbecue. He knew very well what the answer to that question was.

I told him how I almost magically met one person after another who gave me just enough to keep me going. I told him about writing a business plan and making financial projections and going into banks and eating at every barbecue restaurant anywhere in or close to Seattle. I told him about going to Denver and how I was planning to go to Southern Pride to look at the smokers. I told him about the market opportunity I believed to exist in North Seattle.

But mostly I told him I needed him. I needed him to come to Seattle and look at it with me. See firsthand what I was seeing and talk me out of it if I was being crazy. I told him I didn't think I could go any further without him.

Then I paused. There was nothing else to say. I don't know how long I waited for him to say something, but I was aware of my heart racing very fast.

"All right. Sounds like fun."

And that was it. Just that simple. I wrapped it up quickly, promising to be back in touch soon to nail down the details, and then I got off the phone before he could change his mind.

I sat by the phone and tried to breathe normally again. That went pretty well. It wasn't so bad. I guess I shouldn't have made such a big deal about it. It was just a phone call.

But Jesus, why the hell did I have tears in my eyes?

CHAPTER FOURTEEN
June 2004

WHEN I FOUND PETE'S restaurant in Mountlake Terrace and saw it for the first time from the outside, I thought I might have found the spot where my restaurant would be. It looked about the same size as my house, on its own lot, with paved parking that could hold twenty or thirty vehicles. It was on a main road, but a little off from the busier thoroughfare that led to the freeway, where all the traffic flowed with daily downtown commuters. There was a main door into the front of the building for restaurant dining, but also a side door that went directly into the bar, which was a separate section in the rear. I really liked the idea of having a bar. I saw firsthand how Oliver's carried our restaurant, Andaluca. The Dempseys were satisfied if Andaluca broke even every year, which it rarely did. Oliver's, on the other hand, on the strength of its reputation from the Martini Challenge as one of the top cocktail bars downtown, always delivered a healthy profit. Of course, it was booking the hotel rooms that kept us all employed there, but the food and beverage message was clear. Having a popular bar takes good care of the bottom line.

I walked in and immediately saw a big man in the kitchen behind a service counter wearing a dingy white apron, bent over the plates he was preparing for a server waiting on the two or three tables with customers. By the look of his gray hair, haggard expression, and surly demeanor, I assumed this was Pete. A man who definitely looked ready for retirement.

The waitress chirped, "Hi, I'll be right with you. Just yourself tonight?"

"Oh, I just want to speak to the owner for a minute. Thanks."

She looked at the man in the kitchen. "All right." Then she cruised into the dining room.

The old man had overheard us and looked up at me with a suspicious expression.

"Hi, are you Pete?" I wanted to offer a handshake, but the service counter was too high to make that practical, so I just gave him a smile and a nod.

"Yeah?" He nodded back warily.

"I hear your restaurant's for sale. I'm interested."

"What?" He looked around wildly. "Hell no! Who told you that?" He was getting more agitated, craning his neck over the service counter toward the dining room, looking for someone.

I was confused. I thought I was bringing him good news. "Oh. I'm sorry. I guess maybe I got the wrong idea."

"Where did you get it from?"

He was still looking around but was calming down.

"Rocky, from downtown. He said he knows you."

"Wait a minute. I'll talk to you. Let me finish with these orders. Have you got a minute?"

"Sure."

"Just sit down there." He was pointing to a small bench close to the cash register station. "I'll be with you in a minute."

He eyeballed the waitress when she picked up the orders, but she didn't say anything, so he regained his composure. He came out from the kitchen after a few minutes and shook my hand.

"How ya doin'. Listen," he said in a low voice meant for just the two of us, "you gotta be careful about who hears that kind of stuff. My waitress, my dishwasher, my bartender, I don't want them bailin' on me and finding other jobs. You know what I mean?"

"Yeah. I'm sorry. I'm new at this. I didn't think about that."

"So, you know Rocky?"

I told him about talking to Rocky and what my plan was.

"Barbecue, huh? Yeah, that might be pretty good. You wantta do pizza? I could show you how."

"Uh, I don't know if the two things go together that well."

"Well, good luck gettin' that pizza oven out of here. That thing is old and heavier than hell. You'll have to tear down a wall and get it out with a forklift."

I gazed over the service counter at the monster oven he was referring to. BBQ and pizza. I guess I could think about it. In the meantime, I figured we could talk about the bar. After our shaky beginning, Pete was very receptive to me.

I took a tour of the place and told Pete on my way out that I'd give him a call. I wanted to bring Jeff Winter over some time, when the place was closed and nobody else was around, so he could look it over with me. We hadn't talked price, but I figured it didn't really matter yet. If he was ready to get out, and if Jeff could give me a decent cost estimate for turning the place into what I wanted, I would worry about the money later.

John Head was going to be with us for the Fourth of July weekend. My children would be occupied with their mothers and their friends. Leni arranged her schedule so she wouldn't be flying then. She had been invited to a party that was thrown annually on Independence Day on Vashon Island. She was still close with lots of people who lived on the rustic island that was connected to the mainland by a thirty-minute ferry ride across Puget Sound out of West Seattle. We thought John Head might enjoy it. Lots of local eccentric characters would be there. They always roasted a whole pig over an open pit and smoked salmon on cedar planks. It could be a nice diversion while he was with us.

Leni wanted us to throw a party that weekend, too. Maybe a Sunday lunch party that she could invite her local relatives to. She spent the spring and summer digging, pruning, and planting all around our house. She loved being outside and watching her flowers bloom as the summer came on. With her prompting, we cleaned and painted and gave our old, working-class home some admirable curb appeal. She was ready to share the fruits of her labors and her new life with people who had always known her.

I hadn't shared it with Leni yet, but after my meeting with Daniel Petzoldt, I had been mulling over the possibility of selling the house. Daniel had talked about mortgaging my house to the hilt, but I thought it might be better to flip it for a large gain. Lynne was a very good real estate agent and the Seattle market was hot. We could move into a small condo in Mountlake Terrace or Lynnwood that would be closer to where Pete's restaurant was. We could give that mortgage to Daniel Petzoldt's bank. A condo would be easier to maintain, and once the restaurant became successful we could look at selling the condo and buying another house, one that Leni could design as she pleased.

With the cash left over from scaling down, I could put that money in the bank, qualifying for both a line of credit and a business loan to put toward my startup. I didn't know exactly how much it would all add up to, but maybe enough. There was a possibility I could attract another investor, like Tom or Gerry, but I wasn't depending on that. I wanted to be ready to do it all on my own if that was what it took.

Leni would be disappointed to leave our house. She had put a lot of sweat equity into it since she had moved in with me after we married. But this house was part of my old story, who I was before Leni and I were together. Now I was focused on us writing a new story. A story that was uniquely ours and not connected in any way to who we had been previously. She would understand that and be on board with it. I was sure of it.

I would wait until after John Head's visit to broach that subject. First things first. John was coming and we were going to play with his smoker and look at local barbecue places together. After that, I would bring Tom in from Texas to look at what I had, to see if he thought it might work. After those two visits, I expected to be clearer in my mind about whether to keep going or not.

The reason why I was still at the Mayflower Park Hotel, why I was a manager, was because I was loyal and honest. I never skimmed my till as a bartender. Never gave away drinks excessively to sweeten my tips. I never missed shifts, calling in on short notice. I never got into altercations with coworkers or customers, except in the rare instances when I had to cut someone off from having more drinks. I was never in a bad mood at work, never brought my problems behind the bar.

As a manager, I did all I was asked. I was a team player always seeking what was best for the hotel and the employees I supervised. Over the years I had been named employee of the month four times and twice received the award handed out every three months to the most outstanding manager.

I had not studied hospitality management like every other manager in the hotel. I simply learned on the job and did things I was asked to do. And I was valued by Paul Ishii, our general manager, and Steve Johansson, our food and beverage manager, for just that. I was their guy.

So, it was with some sense of guilt that I was working feverishly to see if I could start my own restaurant and get the hell out of there. I felt like I was betraying their trust. They had done everything for me, gave me full support and autonomy to oversee Oliver's without being micromanaged by either of them. Heck, I had been in the hotel twice as long as either of them. They looked to me for a sense of historical perspective, first about the Martini Challenge, and then about employees and managers who predated them.

I didn't like feeling that I was keeping a secret from them. But what could I do? I was a long way from any certainty about going through with it. The whole thing could blow over at any time. If I was going to share my scheme, it would be with Steve J. first. We shared the basement office, were constantly engaged with each other. He could actually be valuable with his opinions and input. Paul, I wouldn't say anything to until I was certain I was going through with it. Once I told him, there would be no turning back.

CHAPTER FIFTEEN
July 2004

JOHN HEAD CAME TO Seattle and we hit the ground running. I hardly let him unpack his bag. It was his first time in Seattle and I made sure he saw almost all of it. I took him to see Pecos Pit, The Steel Pig, The OK Corral, Jones Barbecue. He loved to eat and we tried something everywhere we went. John never missed an opportunity to share with anyone we talked to in these places that he was the director of the Culinary Institute of Smoke-Cooking. No one pressed him for more information than that, just nodded and smiled. I took him to Pete's when I met Jeff Winter there to look the place over. Jeff took measurements and made notes, said he would make a floor plan and an equipment list. He would work up a price estimate for everything we had discussed about what I would be needing.

We looked outside in the back and found a concrete slab that was meant to be used for picnic tables. A shed could be put there to contain a couple of smokers. They could be secured, covered from the elements, and vent naturally in the open air. As I was looking at the place in the light of day, I could see how old and run-down it was, especially the bar area. It could really use some new tables and chairs, and it needed new flooring, new lighting, and new paint on the walls. It went on and on. All that would cost extra money. I wondered if I could start with the place as it was and do all those upgrades gradually.

John Head had chatted briefly with Jeff, but he really went after Pete. He stood in the kitchen with him while Pete was prepping for the evening dinner service. John peppered him with questions about Italian cooking and told him about his own culinary background. Pete looked like he was listening to a sales pitch for something he clearly did not want. At the moment, though, that was Pete's problem.

My concern was more with Jeff Winter. This was the third time I had dragged Jeff out to look at a place with me. The first time had been a strip mall, a rectangular box of a space. He dutifully took his measurements and worked up a floor plan. That place needed lots of plumbing and a grease trap added. There also wasn't very good venting for an indoor smoker. It ended up going nowhere. Then I had him look at a gas station that had closed. That was how Pecos Pit had started downtown, in an old gas station. I saw a similar opportunity at 145th Street and Aurora Avenue in North Seattle. Jeff came and looked it over, but there was no floor plan this time. He said a ton of work would be needed before the health department would even consider granting a license. Now I had him here at Pete's. He was willing to work up a floor plan, he could see the possibilities, but he obviously wasn't very impressed with this aging wreck of a building and the less than stellar Mountlake Terrace location. I could sense Jeff was starting to wonder if this was all getting to be more trouble than it was worth, if I was going to ever deliver a payday for him. He never said anything, was always professional, but something needed to happen soon or I suspected I would begin having a harder time getting Jeff to take or return my calls.

That weekend the weather was perfect when we took John Head over to Vashon Island. The ferry ride, John's first, was smooth and pleasant. We toured the island, looking around at different places Leni led us to, and then we headed over to where the party was going on. As promised, the gathering was uniquely Vashon, men and women who were used to seeing one another and knowing their business on a regular basis. In Texas, they would have been labeled rednecks, but I wasn't sure what the Vashon equivalent to that was. Leni was recognized and greeted openly, mostly by women she had known for years. John and I mostly got some looks and nods when we were introduced, not much more. It was dawning on me that these people didn't only know Leni; they knew her previous husband. He'd grown up out there just like she had. I could only wonder if some of the men looking me over were friends of his, had known him all their lives, like they did Leni. Obviously, they had. I was starting to wonder if coming to this party had been such a great idea.

As Leni was getting more engrossed in catching up with the other women, John and I strolled out toward where the pig roast was. Four or five men stood around the large open pit, the whole pig mounted on a spit and being turned from time to time. They had been there, in different teams, all day and throughout the previous night, drinking beer and tending the cooking. The ones there now, men in their thirties or forties, were looking haggard but satisfied, as the long vigil was coming to a close, with some delicious roasted pork about to be enjoyed by all. We all stood around with a beer in hand, listening as the men chatted easily together. I figured we would watch the pig roast for a while and then go back up to the house. Then John started talking. He was sharing his expertise about the best way to go about roasting a pig, what type of charcoal and wood to use, how to tamp down any flames, what height the pig should be from the coals, how often it should be rotated. The men stopped talking to one another and stared at him as he droned on.

"So…who are you?"

He proudly offered, "I'm John Head, the director of the Culinary Insti…"

"No, what I mean is, who are you? Why are you here? Do you know somebody?"

"Oh." He pointed at me. "I'm with him." They looked at me. That didn't answer the question.

"We're with Leni. I'm her husband."

"Ohhhh…OK." Narrowed eyes, slight smirks. "Leni…yeah." Then they started talking among themselves again.

"Come on, John, let's go grab another beer." No one at that party had any interest in John Head's BBQ pedigree or in anything he wanted to offer about proper pig roasting technique.

When we got back from Vashon Island, we started playing with John's water smoker. We had stopped and picked up some spare ribs and a pork roast. I watched while John showed me how to get it all set up, seasoning the meat and starting to cook it. We sat in the comfortable summer evening on my back porch, drinking a beer, watching the water smoker, talking about barbecue and the differences between Seattle and Denver. The next day, some of Leni's family came over and we served up the meats we had been cooking. They came out moist, tender, and delicious. Our water smoker barbecue was a hit.

When John and I said goodbye, I gave him some money to cover his traveling expenses and told him how much I appreciated that he had come so far across the country to help me. There was still much for me to do, much that still needed to come together, but I couldn't have gotten this far if he had not helped me so generously. I truly hoped I could bring him back, by airplane the next time, to open the restaurant with me. He said he had a good feeling about it and expected to come back. He didn't think I would let myself be stopped. And then he got in his car and drove all the way back to Denver.

Less than a week after John left, something wasn't feeling right to me. His water smoker still sat on my back porch. I hadn't practiced with it since he left. I had no plans to practice with it anytime soon. I wasn't following through with what John intended for me to do. Tom was coming to town soon, less than a couple of weeks. John Head coming to Seattle was supposed to take me up a notch, get me inspired so that when Tom came, I'd be ready to work with him. But that wasn't how I was feeling. Something was missing.

John had a passion for barbecue. He and I could really connect when we were trying some together at different barbecue joints or sitting around the water smoker together, but not when it came to the business of barbecue. John was never much interested in the concept of an automated barbecue smoker. That didn't really mesh with his ideal of how to approach it. For me, everything centered around the inspiration I got when I discovered that smoker. I wasn't interested in being a prize-winning pit master; I was interested in creating a thriving barbecue business that was driven by having technology that made the business efficient and easy to replicate. I wanted to see one of those automated barbecue smokers in action and talk with someone who was doing what I wanted to do. I got an idea of where to start, so I made a phone call.

"Good afternoon, this is Southern Pride, may I help you?" The voice was that of an older woman with a soft and gentle Midwestern accent. I told her I was planning to purchase a couple of the smokers, the smaller ones, and I was interested in talking to someone about them. "We don't sell the smokers here—they're sold by distributors. I can help you contact one in your region."

Right. Jeff Thomas told me he could introduce me to the local rep. That wasn't what my instinct was telling me, though. I asked if there was someone who talked to restaurant owners who were already using the smokers and could connect me with them.

"Hold, please."

"Technical Support, this is Dub." Dub? Was that a nickname? I told him what I wanted.

"We can't give out that kind of information." I explained that I was opening my first barbecue restaurant and I just wanted to learn about the automated smokers from someone already familiar with using them.

"Where are you located? I can refer you to our local distributor." It came back to that again. I took down the name and number for Danny Sizemore, the Northwest rep. I was about to hang up and was finishing the call by saying I still had a lot to learn about the barbecue business and was just hoping to talk with someone who was doing it somewhere else than where I wanted to do it. I figured they wouldn't mind sharing information with me if I wasn't going to be direct competition. He probably didn't get many calls like mine.

"No, not really. We mostly just give technical support. Service calls and such." Then he paused. "You know...now that you mention it, there is a distributor from the southern region who was up here once and was telling us about his son. He was teaching people barbecue from his restaurant in

Tennessee. He worked with a lot of people. One was from England, I think he said, another from New York—folks you wouldn't necessarily think would be doing that. They all went to learn it from him in his restaurant. Place called Backyard Barbecue. In Jackson. The son's name was...uh...Gary. Gary Christian. He might be somebody who could help you."

Now you're talkin', Dub.

CHAPTER SIXTEEN

WHEN TOM ARRIVED IN Seattle, I put the water smoker back to use again. We spent the first pleasantly balmy evening of his visit on my back porch with some tasty ribs and Northwest micro brews. This was the first time in my memory that the two of us were alone together. We were usually with wives, or kids, or Gerry and Mike and their kids, somebody besides ourselves. Leni was flying and wouldn't be joining us until the weekend. My kids were doing their summertime thing with friends. I tried not to mention Maggie; I figured he had about enough of that. There was still some melancholy to him, some sense that he was still missing her in moments worth sharing. But I kept him distracted by completely filling every moment with all things BBQ.

We talked about forming a corporation, opening a business bank account, employee hiring forms and payroll, tax reporting. We probably talked more during that visit, and were more engrossed with what we were talking about together, than in all the rest of our life combined.

I wanted him to see things from the same perspectives I had, so I took him out to meet some people. Our first stop was downtown. "So, this is the brother. The one from Texas." Ed Molzan appraised him from across the table with his mischievous smile. "Well, brother, what do you think? Do you like his barbecue restaurant idea?"

Tom was polite. "He's excited. It's interesting. We'd like to learn more about it."

"Right. Well, he's persistent. I'll give him that." Ed acknowledged that I had learned a lot, that I'd made some good contacts with people who could keep moving me forward. He said I didn't seem to want to take no for an answer, and that was pretty much what it took for someone who was determined to start a small business.

Tom chuckled. "Yeah, that's how he is sometimes. We've seen it before. Like when he went to New York and wanted to be an actor."

Ed's eyes widened. "You? An actor? In New York?" He looked at me incredulously.

"It was a long time ago, Ed," I said. "Ancient history."

"You are full of surprises." He looked at Tom. "Well, at least he's no stranger to facing long odds. You'd better not take him on any trips to Las Vegas with you." Tom just smiled and nodded.

After meeting with Ed, I took Tom over to see Daniel Petzoldt. We showed him the updated business plan Tom had prepared and talked about financing and numbers. Daniel said it was all very exciting and asked Tom if he would be investing. I deflected that by saying I had only sought my brother for his advice and expertise at that point, that any conversations on that subject would come later on, if at all. I just wanted him to meet Daniel to see the outline for the financing we had discussed. So far, this was my baby, not his. Tom didn't say anything.

We went to Bargreen Ellingson and had a meeting with Jeff Winter, looking at all the work he had done and letting Tom ask him some questions. Having Tom there seemed to give me a little more credibility with Jeff. He didn't ask Tom if he was going to be involved financially, but he looked reassured that there was another adult taking me seriously. He hadn't extended that same credibility to John Head when he had met him.

We finished our rounds by going by Pete's to grab some dinner. I casually introduced him to Pete when we came in and mentioned that he was up to visit me from Texas, nothing more that could tip any employees toward suspicion. Tom and I had some pizza, sat in the bar for a drink, and called it an evening. He was able to look into the kitchen on the way out, so when we left, he had a good sense of what Pete's place offered as a location.

Now he had a full grasp of what I was looking at. He had seen everything there was to see on paper, had met everyone who was involved with me in trying to make it happen, except for John Head, but I didn't think that was necessarily a bad thing. John could put people off by pontificating on his barbecue prowess. Now I would give Tom some time to digest all I had deluged him with and then see if he still wanted to work with me on it. There was only one last thing I hadn't shared with him yet, but I wanted to wait until I felt sure about it.

Leni came home, so we spent the next day doing tourist things. We took Tom on a short ferry ride from Edmonds to Kingston, then came back and ate at a nice seafood restaurant by the water. While he was savoring his salmon and clam chowder, he put his first question to Leni. "So, what do you think, Leni? Are you on board with the idea of starting a barbecue restaurant? Isn't that a little outside your experience?"

Leni sighed. "I don't know what to think. He talks like he's just thinking about it, like he doesn't really expect it to happen, and then every time I come back home from a trip, he's telling me he's met someone new. He's got some new thing to tell me or show me. He's learned something that gets him more excited. I don't know. I'm willing to go as far as he wants to. If he really wants to do it, I'll help as much as I can. But you're right, I don't know anything about barbecue. It would be pretty strange. But if I could not have to fly anymore, I'd give it a try. Why not?"

"Well, that's the thing, he doesn't know anything about barbecue either." He looked at me. "I know you've met that man from Denver who's an expert, or claims to be an expert, but it's a pretty long stretch to think he's going to get you fully prepared to operate a barbecue restaurant in the week or two before you plan to open. He only cares about how you cook the food. And then he's out of there."

"Yeah," I said, "I think you're right."

Tom shrugged. "You've met some interesting people and you've put a lot of work into it. I think you could do it. I believe you could. But I don't think you should try it right now, not until you've had a lot more time to really learn about the business. I think you should probably be more patient."

Now I needed to tell him that last thing. "I've met a man who's going to let me come study his barbecue restaurant for a solid week. A restaurant that has been in operation for fourteen years. A barbecue restaurant in Jackson, Tennessee."

Tom and Leni both stopped eating and stared at me. "He uses Southern Pride smokers, just like the ones I want to use. He has a full restaurant that seats over one hundred and fifty. He has a full staff of employees. He's going to show me how they prep, how they cook, how they serve. He's going to answer any questions I have about how the ovens operate, about catering, about employees, about equipment, about anything I want to know about the business."

Leni chirped, "Am I going?"

"Oh yes, we're using your flight benefits to get there. And you're going to learn everything that I learn."

Tom asked, "Where did you meet this man?"

"I found him through a contact at Southern Pride. We talked on the phone and he was very receptive to me."

"And why is that?" Tom pressed. "Why is he so eager to show you everything about his restaurant?"

"Because I am going to pay him."

I might have exaggerated a bit. I did find Gary Christian. I did talk to him on the phone. He did tell me a little about his restaurant and that he did indeed provide barbecue consulting for prospective restaurateurs. He'd only assured me of an immersive experience in the daily operation of a barbecue restaurant. That after a week of being around his place, I would know exactly what I was getting myself into. I would have no illusions; nothing would be sugarcoated. If I wanted to truly learn how a successful barbecue business operated, he had one to show me.

I'd asked him if he could provide me with some references, some former clients he had consulted with who went on to start their own restaurants. I was interested in calling them to ask about the experiences they had with him and how their barbecue places were doing. He provided two. One was a man from Michigan. The other were a married couple in Nebraska. The man in Michigan was hard to get on the phone; he never seemed to be around. When I did finally catch him, he only gave me a few minutes. He said the training was everything he expected it to be, that he'd learned a lot, though he said he'd expected Gary would have spent more time with him than he actually did. He had gotten his first restaurant going and was now working on opening his second. Business was good, but it was way more work than he thought it would be, and employees were a headache. You had to find good people, he said, and that was not easy. The woman I talked to in Nebraska also said they had no regrets about working with Gary. Their restaurant, which had previously been a Dairy Queen, was less busy than that of the man in Michigan. They were struggling a little bit to gain customers because there was more competition than they had realized. She felt they still had a good chance of making it, but it would take some time. They would need to be patient. She admitted, like the man in Michigan, that it was a lot of work.

I'd found all this out in the week before Tom came to visit. I hadn't yet sent Gary my deposit check and I hadn't shared any of this information with Leni. I was at a crossroads. In all my time pursuing the siren call of an automated barbecue smoker, throughout all the people I met and all the things I learned, this was the first time I was being called upon to put some serious money where my mouth was. And I was betting it all on a maybe. Maybe I'd get the knowledge I needed to give me the confidence to open my own place. Maybe, after betting my home and everything else I owned, I'd have just enough money to take one decent swing at it. Maybe I'd get Pete's place. Maybe I'd leave my secure, steady job to do this thing. And for every one of those maybes, there was a maybe not. There were all kinds of potential stumbling blocks before me.

That was why I hadn't yet told Tom about Gary Christian. That was why I hadn't made a decision. I knew taking that step meant I wasn't just playing with this idea anymore. I was making a financial commitment to it.

Tom had nailed it when he said I was too dependent on what I was counting on from John Head. In that moment, I knew I had lost both him and Leni. They would treat me gently, try not to hurt my feelings, but there would be no more serious consideration of doing anything. They would tell me to let it go and move on. They would say it was time for me to walk away.

And that was the moment I committed. We were going to Tennessee. I might go down in flames, but I refused to let my dream die in a cozy corporate restaurant booth with a nice view of the water. I was going to go find out what made Backyard Barbecue tick. And after that, I hoped that whatever else I was supposed to do next would become clear. And that whatever it was, Leni and Tom would still be doing it with me.

"So, you think you'll learn enough in one week to come back and open your own restaurant?"

Tom was looking at me searchingly, critically. Leni, contemplating the prospect of training in a barbecue restaurant across the country in someplace she had never heard of, was looking at me in shock.

"I'll tell you what. I believe I'll learn enough in one week to come back and be absolutely certain whether I'll do it or not. And I fully intend to do it. If I do, will you help me?"

Tom glanced at Leni, the nice water view, and back at me. "Yes. Of course. I'll do everything I can to help you."

I smiled at Leni. "Does Alaska fly to Tennessee?"

"Oh Lord," she said. "Oh, my Lord."

CHAPTER SEVENTEEN

TOM'S LAST DAY WITH us was a Sunday and he wanted to go to church. He was still devout in his Catholicism, which he had converted to for Maggie. Keeping his faith by attending mass was a way for him to maintain her memory, to have hope for their spirits to meet again when his time eventually came.

We both put on some dark slacks and button-down dress shirts and posed outside in the front doorway for Leni to snap a picture of us together. We got in the car and drove downtown to St. James Cathedral, a venerable jewel of Seattle's oldest churches, and caught the morning mass. I sat respectfully, going through the rituals with them. In silence, I prayed with gratitude for Tom's visit, hoping that it was as special for him as it was for me, that I wasn't being a fool with all this BBQ craziness, for guidance in going to Tennessee. I was feeling increasingly that there was something, or the spirit of someone, who was working in concert with me, that my Guardian Angel was there to oversee and keep me protected. My mother? My father? It was too preposterous to fully embrace. Yet, I was filled with a sense of spirit within and around me.

When the service was over, I felt good we had come; I felt at peace. We got in the car and I started driving us back up to Shoreline. Heading north on I-5, something clicked in my mind that I remembered from when we had our meeting with Jeff Winter. We had been sitting around a table talking, and I was stating yet again that starting a barbecue restaurant in the north end was an opportunity because no one else had gotten there yet.

Jeff said, "Yeah, well, not for long. I heard that Jones Barbecue is looking to open in Lake Forest Park. That's right next to Shoreline. You guys better get on it. I'm sure somebody else will get the same idea if Jones does well out there."

"Lake Forest Park?"

"Yeah, there's some kind of mall out there, on the way to Kenmore and Bothell. They call it a town center, I think. There's a big bookstore, Third Place Books."

I had forgotten all about it after we left the meeting.

"You know, we've got some time, I'm going to take a swing up Lake City Way. There's something I want to see."

Tom said, "I'm ready for breakfast."

"Sure, we can find someplace going that way. I just want to take a look at something."

I had been dragging Tom around the city for days looking at closed restaurant spaces and empty strip mall units. I showed him the closed gas station I had taken Jeff Winter to see. He thought we were through with that part of the trip.

Lake City was not an area I came through frequently, and when we went beyond 145th Street and the road turned into Bothell Way, I had only a vague recollection of seeing this part of Seattle before.

"Do you know where we're going?" Leni asked.

"Umm. I don't know. I'll know it when I see it."

"Breakfast," Tom repeated.

"Soon," I replied.

After passing through a traffic light, there was a row of stores that came up on the left and a large parking lot. Driving by, I saw more stores set back farther from the road, and then a large sign at an entrance for Third Place Books. I took the next left and circled back into the parking lot.

"What's here?" Tom asked.

"This is the place Jeff was talking about the other day, where he said Jones Barbecue was going in. I just want to see what it looks like. It won't take long."

We got out of the car and went into the main entrance, where the bookstore sign was. When we entered there were some small shops, a public library, but no bookstore that I could see. There also was no barbecue place.

Leni said, "It's in here? I don't see anything."

I said, "No, I don't see anything either. Looks like a weird spot to put a restaurant. Maybe I got it wrong. Never mind, let's go find someplace to eat."

But Tom had noticed an escalator up ahead of us. He'd stepped onto it and was going up.

"Where's he going?" Leni asked.

"I don't know. There's more upstairs, I guess. Maybe that's where the bookstore is."

We followed and went up the escalator behind him. We came off into the bookstore. There were more main doors on the other side that opened into another large parking lot. More stores were also back there. I couldn't see that from driving by on Bothell Way.

To the right was a bakery cafe. It was bustling, with a line of customers, mostly waiting to order espresso coffee drinks, a raging fad that had become entrenched in Seattle in the years since I had arrived there. Stretching around from the bakery was a row of food-court storefronts. There was a Japanese restaurant, a pizza joint, a Mexican restaurant. They faced a very large seating area of tables and chairs, enough to accommodate dozens, maybe three or four hundred people. Some of the tables were cafe style, where two to four could sit, but some were long and rectangular, so that several people could sit around them together. Then, at the far end, beyond the tables, was a large stage with a podium on it that someone could speak from.

I didn't really identify all that at first. That came later, when I took the whole place in. The first thing that riveted my attention was the storefront next to the bakery. It was set apart from the other restaurants that ran in a row behind it. It was situated so that it was prominent to see whether you came from the back parking lot or from the escalator, as we had.

It was dark and empty, looking like it had been closed for a long time. It was a diner, designed in an art deco kind of way, like something from the '50s, something akin to a setting on the TV show *Happy Days*.

"What's this?" Tom asked. "Looks like it's closed."

I walked up, giving it a closer look. It was dark, but you could see it had everything. Sinks for dish washing, food prepping, hand washing. A mop closet, a full hood for smoke ventilation. There were refrigerators, a soda fountain, deep fryers, a char broiler. There was even a cash register on the counter. It was almost turn-key, like I could practically roll in my automated barbecue smokers, turn on the lights, and be ready for business. At least it felt that way.

Tom said, "This could work."

Leni said, "It's cute."

A voice from behind called out, "Hey! What are you doing here?"

I turned to see a longtime regular from Oliver's, a guy I had known for years. His name was Vince, and he was one of the old-time Seattleites. We called him Big-Nose Vince, not only because he had the physical attribute for it, but because he was a guy who loved to nose into other people's business. He was looking us over with a big smile, sensing that he was on to something juicy.

"Oh, hi, Vince. You from around here?"

"Yeah, I come through here all the time. I live up in Kenmore. You lookin' at this old space? It was Al's Diner. It's been closed for months. Are you interested in it? Ha?" he said, still grinning at me while glancing at Leni and Tom.

I introduced him to them, said I was looking at it. I had an idea for a restaurant and was interested in finding a location it could work in.

"What kind of restaurant? Something with hamburgers? That's what they were mostly doing here, hamburgers and french fries, that sort of thing." Vince was a bigmouth. If I told him what I was doing and to keep it a secret, I could count on him making a beeline to Oliver's to announce it loudly as something only he was privy to. Still, I was growing weary of guarding my secret so closely. Maybe it was time to own it. "Well, Vince, I'm thinking about a barbecue restaurant. I don't know for sure I'm going to do it, though. I very well may not when it's all said and done. But I think something like that could work well in a place like this."

He nodded with enthusiasm. "Wow! You know how to make barbecue?"

Tom chuckled and ambled away toward the bakery.

"Oh, that's right, you're from Texas! Oh yeah, I guess you learned it down there, huh? Sure, that would be something new here."

"I thought I heard something about Jones Barbecue coming in here. Have you heard that?"

"No, I haven't. But you know who you should talk to is Robert. He's the manager of the bookstore. They lease all this space. All the food places rent from them. Except HoneyBear, the bakery. They own that." I looked over into the bookstore. "Here, let me see if I can find him. I'll introduce you. He's who you should talk to, for sure. He's the one who's in control." Vince scurried off to find him. He was in his comfort zone, seeing himself as an insider, the go-between bringing movers and shakers together. It just figured I would run into him here.

"You know him?" Leni asked.

"Not really. I just know who he is from work."

"Is he going to tell people you want to leave your job?"

"I don't think he'll put it that way. But he'll certainly blab about what I'm doing. I might need to start talking about it myself soon anyway."

She looked concerned. "Well, I hope you don't lose your job over it. Not yet anyway."

"I'm not going to lose my job. It'll be all right."

Vince came back from his hunt. "He's not there—he's on vacation. He won't be back for a couple of weeks."

"A couple of weeks?"

"Yeah. Oh well. I tried to get some information from somebody else over there, but they just told me you would have to talk to Robert. He's the only one dealing with the restaurants. Nobody else knows anything."

I thanked Vince and walked over to where Tom stood by the bakery, munching a maple bar.

"You ready?"

"I like this place. We could eat here."

"No, I don't think so." I glanced back at Vince, looking after us with his ingratiating grin. "I think it's time to go for now." I gave one more look at Al's Diner and remembered my prayer at St. James, wondering if this spot was destined to be my answer from above. "But I will be back."

I dropped Tom off at SeaTac to catch his flight home, assuring him we would see each other again soon. I was not talking about him making a return trip to help me open the restaurant. I felt he was sure that day would never come. He didn't say it; what he said was that he was going to file for my corporate status as soon as he got home. He'd continue developing the files for handling all the bookkeeping and accounting, get me all set up, just like I was another one of the businesses he represented as a CPA. That's what he said.

And that will be the end of it, I imagined him thinking.

When I said we would see each other soon, I meant at South Padre Island. The family was gathering down there at the end of the summer. Gerry and Mike would be there, as would Tom and all my nieces and nephews. It would be my best chance to have everyone in the family with whom I wanted to share my barbecue plan in one place at the same time. If my plan was dead by then, Leni and I could just enjoy the beach. Tom and I would keep it our little secret and life would get back to normal.

But, if it wasn't dead, I was hoping to share the exciting news with the family to see if there was any interest among them in either getting involved in some way or investing some money in it. I didn't seriously believe I would get one or the other, but I could entertain the possibility of getting some enthusiastic support, some *Yeah! You go, boy!* Later, once they saw some evidence of me having a measure of success down the road, well, then there could maybe be some of either. Having them just be supportive of me would mean a lot.

CHAPTER EIGHTEEN

LAKE FOREST PARK WAS a sleepy suburban community, primarily residential, on the northern edge of King County, close to Lake Washington. It had been founded in the early twentieth century by a developer who saw the area as a pristine location of rolling hills and forest, with the sprawling lake to enjoy as well.

It stayed a sleepy community of mostly family homes tucked away among the trees or close to the lakeside for many years. Then, in the early '60s, real estate development in Seattle started rapidly moving north. When it was learned that a seventeen-acre plot of land close to the lake was going to be used for a new shopping center, the majority of residents voted for incorporation. Lake Forest Park became a town, so that it could exercise some control over the amount of development that would occur inside its borders.

They later came to appreciate having the new shopping center as the commercial hub of the city. And that was the Lake Forest Park Town Center we discovered that day when we went looking for Jones Barbecue.

I went back again and again. I found out that the massive seating area was called The Commons. The principal owner of Third Place Books and HoneyBear bakery, a man named Ron Sher, had leased and redeveloped practically the entire upper level of the town center in the late '90s.

The people of Lake Forest Park embraced the new enterprise when it opened to the public as if they had found water in the desert. Besides the town center, there just wasn't much else going on around there. As my father always preached, Ron Sher had found something to provide Lake Forest Park that wasn't there but was needed.

Not long after the grand opening, he was standing in a long line of people waiting to be served at Honey Bear, moaning to a friend that he wasn't sure what to do about the cavernous space still left, far more than was practical for just seating customers. Eavesdropping behind him in that line was Ann Stadler, an elderly, longtime resident of the area and an unabashed buttinski. She immediately and plainly told him what the people of Lake Forest Park wanted. And the idea of The Commons came into being.

With the food court framing two sides and the stage and bookstore edging along the other two, The Commons allowed for crowds to assemble. They could eat and drink, read, or socialize. The stage was constantly in use for author presentations, community meetings, performances by local schools and cultural groups, with live bands providing music on the weekends.

The thriving hub served Ron Sher's stated mission perfectly. It was the third place, a place besides home and work. A place where people wanted to be.

The more I saw it, the more I liked it. I got to check out the Al's Diner space more closely and came to learn that all the equipment in the space was still in good working order, available for use if a new tenant wanted to take advantage of it. With all the plumbing, electrical, counters, and flooring alone, I could save thousands in start-up costs, probably tens of thousands. Not to mention using some of the appliances already there. This was a unique opportunity.

I kept nosing around, asking for Robert, but he was never there. I couldn't get anyone to tell me anything about Jones Barbecue coming. All I got was that I would have to talk to Robert, and he wouldn't be back for a while. There wasn't any sign announcing Jones Barbecue was coming. Maybe the deal hadn't gone through. Maybe it was just a rumor. I was afraid that I was going to get myself all worked up about the possibilities, only to be in for a huge letdown when Robert finally showed up and told me the space was already leased to Jones. Something kept nagging at me to keep trying, keep looking for this Robert guy.

I visited Pete from time to time, just to keep that iron in the fire. I think Pete and I both knew by then that his place wasn't really what I wanted, although I continued to believe it might work if it was the best option I could ultimately come up with. He liked me, though, and the more I saw him, the more he became somewhat of a confidant; someone I could talk plainly with about what I was hoping to do. He liked hearing my plans, would ask me questions about the food and the cooking techniques involved. Talking with Pete helped me clarify a sense of purpose. I felt like I was becoming clear on what I wanted to do with barbecue. I just needed to learn more about how to do it.

And that's where Gary Christian came in. I was wearing him out with emails: confirming that he'd received my deposit, pushing to guarantee a date for me to come in August, asking for advice on where to stay, asking for clear directions on how to get to Jackson and find Backyard Barbecue. This man I had never met was now emerging as the person finally deciding whether this would really happen or not. One week, actually only Monday through Friday, would determine my fate. Leni and I were to be thrown into it, left to fend for ourselves as we trailed the employees and got hands-on experience as much as we could be comfortable with taking on. I was more than a little intimidated at the prospect. When we talked on the phone, Gary sounded upbeat and nonchalant, like I was just another in a long line of tenderfoots that was coming to him for help. "Oh, it'll be fine," he boomed at me. "Y'all will pick it up in no time. I'll be here to answer any questions for you, and I've got some people who have been with me a long time. They'll take good care of you. You don't have nothin' to worry about."

I wasn't worried. Just a little apprehensive. Would I be the most tender-footed tenderfoot he'd ever worked with? Would he be taken aback at how little I knew about the most commonsense concepts of barbecue? Regardless, I was quite sure of one thing. I was going to get my money's worth.

These people were more than halfway across the country and didn't know me or Leni in the least. We could be as stupid as a post and once we left at the end of the week, it wouldn't matter to anyone there anymore. Or even if it did, and we ended up being the most famous boneheads to ever pass through Jackson, Tennessee, we would never have to hear about it. So, I planned to stick my nose into every corner of that place and ask anything that popped into my head at any time. And when I left there I would either be ready to come back to Seattle and open a barbecue restaurant, or else I would know exactly why I would never do that.

Gary confirmed we were booked for the third week in August. We were set. It was happening. Now I could get Leni to arrange a flight for us. I could book a rental car and an inexpensive motel to stay in. There was only one detail in arranging the trip that I was a little uncomfortable with. Telling Steve Johansson I needed another week off from work.

It was pretty short notice and he would expect me to give some kind of reason for it. I could make something up or I could man up and tell the truth. I was never good at being disingenuous and I had never been that way with any of my bosses at the hotel. I thought I could address it with Steve in a way that would ensure him that I wasn't going to do anything rash, that I was only testing the waters. Besides, if Big-Nose Vince came into Oliver's anytime soon, the cat would be out of the bag anyway. I'd rather he heard it from me than getting it as a rumor.

What if he didn't approve me going away for a week? What if it was too short notice and he already had plans of his own that precluded me being gone? Would I bag the trip to Tennessee? Would I bag my whole barbecue venture? Would I quit my job? Lots of weighty questions, but I just knew, one way or another, I was going to Tennessee.

I invited Lynne over to our house to give us an appraisal.

"Why are you selling? Are you two wanting to find your dream house together?" she asked.

"Not quite, Lynne. It's more to do with a strategy in starting my own business."

"Your own business! Really? What are you going to do?"

As usual, my reply was shortly followed by her incredulously asking, "You know how to make barbecue?"

Once we were through talking about the peculiarities of my plans, she posed a more striking question. "Do Hannah and Kyle know you're doing this?"

My children, in fact, did not know. It wasn't really that I was keeping it a secret from them, although I wasn't particularly interested in getting any blowback from either of their mothers if or when they came into the circle of knowledge. Not that I thought the women would care what I was doing one way or the other. But, in the interest of uninterrupted child support payments, they might be tempted to weigh in on the rationality of my obsession with automated barbecue smokers.

"I'm waiting to tell the kids until I'm sure it will really happen. At this point, nothing's definite. It's not even definite we're going to sell the house. I just want to have everything in place to do it if we decide to pull the trigger on it. What I would like to do is sell the house for as much as we can get for it, and then turn around and buy the cheapest condo we can find. We want to own something for the investment and mortgage interest tax write-off, but I want to pull as much money out as I can to be available to use in the business if I need it."

"OK, we can do that. Prices are going up, but I think we can still find some deals if we go north. Maybe Lynnwood or Mountlake Terrace. There are still some values out there. We can make that work."

"I'll leave it all to you and Leni to find a place you like. I want a place Leni will be happy with. If we start the business, I don't plan to be there much in the beginning anyway."

She looked at Leni and enthused, "Us girls will find a good place for you. We'll have fun, won't we, Leni?"

Leni looked at my ex-girlfriend's sister and gave her best flight-attendant smile. "We sure will."

I checked in with Daniel Petzoldt to let him know I was making plans for selling my house and using the capital gain toward the business. "Great! Let's get your accounts started for checking and savings. When you find the property you want to move into, we'll get your mortgage set up here. At that point we should be able to see exactly what we can approve for a business loan and an equity line of credit."

Sound Community Bank was going to own me.

"HEY STEVE, CAN WE talk for a minute?"

"Sure, what's up?"

I waited until the end of the day to corner him, when we were alone in our basement office. There were no more issues in front of him and he was winding down, changing his shoes before making the trip home. He had grown up and always resided on Bainbridge Island, making the ferry commute back and forth to the city most of his adult life for his job. He had that ferry-commuter instinct of always being aware of the next sailing. I knew I had about ten minutes, and then, no matter whether I was about to reveal the secret to eternal happiness, he'd be out the door: *Tell me tomorrow—gotta make the ferry.*

I started slowly, explaining how I had the seed of an idea from having found the automated barbecue smoker. I gave him the whole story up to that point. I felt like I just had to play it out a little longer. I needed to go to Tennessee, find out what I could learn there. I would know after that trip if I was still serious or not. I loved my job and I wouldn't leave it for anything in the world, except this bizarre possibility of starting a business of my very own. I just wanted his support in taking it as far as I could. He just stared at me for several seconds. "I've gotta go." He grabbed his bag and made for the door, stopping and turning back just before he went out. "Does Paul know?"

"No, not yet. You first. Him only if I'm sure."

"Good. Good. We'll talk tomorrow." He started to go again, but turned back once more. "You need an investor?"

"Uhh…yeah…maybe…. I hadn't really considered that yet."

"We'll talk tomorrow." Then he was gone. And I thought I was dropping a bombshell on *him.*

CHAPTER NINETEEN
August 2004

"HELLO, I'M ROBERT SINDELAR."

I finally found my man at Third Place Books. We shook hands and I noted he was close to a generation younger than me. He looked serious, erudite, completely befitting the manager of a sprawling bookstore with a sizable number of employees. He was polite, but no-nonsense. He came right to the point. "I understand you've been here several times looking for me, that you are interested in the Al's Diner space. I'm sorry, but it's probably not available."

Probably; that's what I'd heard.

"I'm not surprised to hear that, but since we've met, let me tell you a little bit about myself and what I would like to do. I live in the area here and this is an idea that I am very passionate about. If the circumstances happen to change and an opportunity develops, I'd like you to have me in mind as an alternative."

"Fair enough. Let's sit down for a few minutes."

We went into The Commons and found a spot to sit across from each other, a large skylight in the ceiling above washing us in a pale afternoon light. I told him again that because I lived in the area, I felt like I had more of a personal desire for creating a restaurant that appealed to people around there. They were my neighbors, people I would see when I went to the grocery store, the post office, the bank. I told him about my strong background in food and beverage and that I had a passion for good barbecue, something I had learned from growing up with it in Texas. I tried to impress upon him that I had a solid business plan and had financing lined up through Sound Community Bank. I wanted the Al's Diner space because so much of it was already done and available. It would take a lot of financial pressure off me in starting my first place.

"Yeah, and that's not all," he said casually. "Because we operate Honey-Bear, we decided to go ahead and provide dishes for the whole food court. We have work staff who clear and maintain the tables, taking the dishes back to an area to wash them and then recirculate them among the restaurants. They also clean and maintain the restrooms. It's all included in the rent. So is water and garbage."

This place was too good to be true.

"I don't want to take up any more of your time. I just want you to know I'm really serious about this. I'm going to do it, if not here, somewhere else in the area. But I think it could work ideally in a place like this, give people here something new and exciting to choose."

"I appreciate that, but like I said, it looks like we already have something in the pipeline. There are just some final details to be worked out. I wish you lots of luck, though."

"Well, if you don't mind, I'm going to continue to check in with you every now and then. Just in case. If your something falls through, I would like the chance to be considered."

We stood up and shook hands one more time in parting. "That's fine. I'll tell Ron about you. If there is any chance for you, it would be his call. He'd have to meet you."

"That would be great. Thanks for your time." Once again, I had tried to build myself up with a lot of blather. It wasn't ego; I wasn't trying to impress him. I just desperately wanted him to take me seriously. Jones Barbecue already had two or three locations. They were long established in Seattle. I was nobody. At this point I had done nothing. I was just a talker. Like the old expression: All hat, no horse.

It didn't look like I had much of a chance there, but if the deal with Jones Barbecue was done, why hadn't Robert even mentioned their name? Why wasn't there some kind of "Coming Soon" sign on the Al's Diner space? I felt like there was something still keeping the door open just a crack. Robert did not out and out tell me no. He did not tell me to just go away. He said he would tell Ron Sher about me. If I could get in front of Ron Sher, there was still a chance.

STEVE JOHANSSON GAVE ME his full support. He wished he could do something like it as well. He had done some probing of his own to see if he could start a restaurant. The concept he had in mind was more Northwest, more associated with fusing culinary styles of what was popular and took advantage of pairing well with wines. Of course, he wanted a full bar providing cutting-edge cocktails. He wanted to open something over on Bainbridge Island. There were sophisticated, discriminating tastes among many of the local inhabitants that he felt he could tap into. Plus, he was a native son, he knew lots of people over there. He had already shared his ideas with our chief engineer, the director of maintenance for the hotel. Susil was originally from Sri Lanka and had years of experience in maritime engineering on ships around the world.

I have no idea how Paul Ishii recruited him to come work at the Mayflower Park. I just know that Susil welcomed the chance to work on shore for once. He was incredibly good at his job. He transformed the engineering department in the basement next to our office into a completely up-to-date and meticulously organized department. He helped the hotel in taking on and completing major renovations in plumbing and upgrading of the elevators. He was, from the Dempseys' standpoint, Paul Ishii's best hire and most valuable manager. He apparently had also socked away a lot of cash over the years. He wasn't one to put too much reliance in financial advisors; he preferred to call his own shots. As he listened to Steve J wax poetically about the restaurant he wished he could open, he piped up that he could back him, be a silent investor. He had no interest in having to work in the restaurant in any way. He only liked the idea of cashing in on a share of the profits. Oh, and maybe being able to come in with his family whenever he wanted to be groveled to.

When Steve J got the skinny from me about what I wanted to do, he immediately thought about Susil. "I don't know that I will get anything going on with my idea anytime soon. Probably not. It'll have to wait until I retire maybe. But Susil is definitely interested in investing in a restaurant. He's a possibility for you."

"Well, I'll talk to him. No harm in that. Will he keep it quiet?"

"Oh sure, he's discreet. We'll just tell him to keep it to himself and he'll be fine. He's not a big talker." Steve was out the door to fetch him. Why was he so eager to bring Susil in? I hadn't really thought through the angle of having an investor. I knew it could help, but it also meant I no longer had full control. There was someone else I had to answer to. If Susil had money to spare, it could make the difference between just scraping by or maybe really going big with a high-volume operation. There would be money for marketing and advertising, for hiring experienced professionals.

Steve came back with Susil in tow behind him. "Steve says you have an exciting idea. What are you doing?"

This was weird—I wasn't expecting this at work—but I decided to go with it, though. "Susil, I have an idea for a barbecue restaurant."

"Barbecue! Sounds good. What's that?" His look was frank. He was serious.

"Well, it's like smoked meats. Brisket and pork and ribs. Cooked at a low temperature over several hours."

"Oh, yeah! I've seen that. Like in the South. Like cowboys."

"Right. Like in the South. Right. Well, it's getting popular all over the place. Even up here. There are people that really like it, seek it out. I mean, people are moving around all over the country now, right? They're coming to Seattle, but they miss the kind of food they knew from where they were from. Or even if they grew up in Seattle and don't know much about barbecue, they've heard about it. They're curious."

"Yeah, I'm curious." He looked at Steve J, and Steve nodded his head enthusiastically. "You know where you want to do this? You have a place?"

"Not yet. I have a couple of possibilities I'm considering, but I haven't definitely decided yet."

"Well, I'd like to learn more, maybe see where you want to start your restaurant. I'm interested, but I'm not a fool. Restaurants can be risky. I have to feel good about it."

"Sure. I would want you to."

"Steve likes what you're doing. I want to learn more. Maybe we can do business."

"Well, I'm going to Tennessee to do some more research and get some ideas on how I want to set up my own place. I'll get back to you after I do that."

"Good. We can talk. I might be interested. I'm looking for an investment. I would want a fair return on my money."

"Of course." I looked at Steve and he was smiling at me. I wasn't sure if he was giving me encouragement or just enjoying watching me squirm.

"All right, I'll talk to you again when you can give me more information. Thank you."

Man, I did not see that coming. Maybe having Susil with me could make a difference down the road. I'd have to figure it out later. Things were beginning to move pretty fast now. But I had to admit, it was kind of exciting. It was starting to feel like something might really be happening.

I CALLED ROBERT AND told him I was just checking in to see if he had any news.

"No, nothing yet."

"I'm heading to Tennessee this weekend. I'll give you one more call before I go and if there's still nothing, I'll check again when I get back."

"Sounds good. Have a good trip."

He wasn't giving me anything to build my hopes on, but he also wasn't telling me it was over. By the time I got back from Tennessee it might not matter anyway. This trip was looming like a giant hammer over my head. I was trying not to let my insecurities gain too much control of my thoughts. It was easy to build the trip up as a make or break event. The scary part was that I had no control. Leni and I would have to just show up and trust these people I did not know at all to give us the knowledge and hands-on experience we needed to really have the confidence to risk practically everything we owned on a hunch I got from glancing at a magazine. The good news, I guess, was that for only three thousand dollars I would verify what a fool I was being and stop this silliness. The better news would be that I would come back to Seattle and I would do it. I would really do it. I had come too far to back down now. I had to give it my best shot.

Back at the hotel, I found that Steve J was curious to know everything I would tell him about what I had done and was going to do. He wanted to know all about the trip to Tennessee, what I was expecting to gain from it. I had friends on the waitstaff in Oliver's that I talked to every day. Slowly, I was leaking the news that I was exploring the possibility of opening my own barbecue restaurant. I knew that it was going to start coming out eventually and I wanted to be the one to share it with the people there who had known me the longest. I still wasn't saying anything to Paul Ishii. That would come after I went to Tennessee, after I knew I was committed to keep going with it. The news was taken by all with surprise and excitement for me, although I could sense some bemusement. A barbecue restaurant? In Seattle? It wasn't unheard of, but, why you? After years of working in a classy environment that was respected for good taste and quality, you want to open a greasy rib joint?

I couldn't really explain it to them or myself. It had something to do with reclaiming my roots, I think, reclaiming a Texas family I had separated from at a young age to chase dreams of being an actor in New York City. Those dreams had ultimately not worked out and now this dream of creating a successful business with my brother had resurrected a hope in me that there was still something worthwhile I could accomplish. None of that was really clear in my mind; it was what lurked within me on a more subconscious level. I appreciated what I had at the hotel, but it felt like I had to do something else that no one who knew me there could really understand.

CHAPTER TWENTY

LENI AND I WERE early getting to the airport to catch our flight to Tennessee. We stopped at Thirteen Coins to have some breakfast before she took her car over to the employee parking lot. We were trying to take advantage of Leni's employee status as much as we could. She had put us on standby for two flights—one to Memphis, the other to Nashville. Both of them were close to full and it would be tight for us to get seats. But we had usually been able to make it whenever we flew standby. There always seemed to be a couple of seats because of people not showing up. We were cautiously optimistic this time would work out as well.

At breakfast we went over the plans we had for when we arrived. We would be very busy getting to Jackson from either Memphis or Nashville and settled into where we would stay. The next day we would jump right into the fire. I was excited and ready to go get started. Leni was more relaxed, hoping we would also take advantage of seeing some sights in Tennessee, maybe do some non-BBQ-related activities. Business first, I said, tourist stops after. The only trip I had in mind outside of Jackson was a run up to Marion, Illinois to visit Southern Pride. They said we could drop by anytime. It was only a couple hundred miles from Jackson, passing briefly across Kentucky and Missouri. Then I could get some up-close and personal time in with an automated barbecue smoker, and with someone who could hold my hand and walk me through what these machines were all about.

At the airport the first flight we were holding out for was to Memphis. It quickly became apparent we weren't going to get on. Nashville was our only shot. We had to white-knuckle it for a couple of hours. It was going to be a close one, down to the final boarding call. I was nervous, but I knew we would somehow get on that plane. We had to. The only other alternative we had for leaving that day was to fly into Atlanta. That flight wasn't leaving until the evening and would get in late that night. Atlanta was hours away from where we wanted to be. It would have us miss a whole day of our schedule just getting there. It would cost us more for the car and then we would also have to spend more time getting back to Atlanta to get home again. It was not a good alternative.

We sat close to the gate watching the passengers boarding and waited with increased anxiety. People kept arriving to check in; no standbys were being called. Then one was called, then another couple. We were next; they just needed to call it out.

And then they closed the passageway door. The flight was closed. We missed it.

I couldn't believe it. I was devastated. We had to make that flight. I should have just bought us tickets instead of counting on standby.

"What are we going to do?" Leni asked.

"Well, I guess we have to go to Atlanta."

"That's hours away. I don't want to hang out here. Let's go home. We can come back later."

I was having a hard time moving.

"C'mon, let's go home," she said gently.

We hadn't checked our bags, so we wheeled them back out to the arrivals area.

"I'll go get the car," she said. "I'll pick you up outside. You take the bags with you."

She started down to the end of the terminal to catch an employee bus to the parking lot. I went outside and stood with the luggage, watching people coming and going from the busy terminal. It was a good summer morning, some clouds, but nothing ominous. I could see the sun starting to shine through from behind puffy pillows of white. But my mood was nowhere near as sunny.

This was not good. We'd be playing catch-up to cram in what we needed to learn. I was questioning again whether I should persist in forcing this trip, this whole venture, to happen.

Once again, as I gazed at the beautiful sky, I reached out with a prayer.

"I don't know. Maybe this is a mistake. I've only lost five hundred dollars so far. Should I pull the plug? Should I just forget it? Am I trying too hard to make this happen? I've done everything I can think of. I don't know what else I can do. It's in your hands. Help me to do whatever it is I need to do next. Please."

And I just listened. I was in a reverie, lost in the clouds. Then I heard my name.

What? My name? It was Leni's voice calling me. I turned and she was hurrying toward me. I had only left her a few minutes ago.

"I got us a flight!"

I was stunned into silence.

"I was going down the terminal, trying to think of some other airline that could get us somewhere closer. I was almost at the end and then I saw this woman at the Southwest Airlines counter. I don't know why I even thought about it, but I just went over and asked her did she have anything going close to Tennessee."

"We have a flight to Nashville. It's leaving in about half an hour."

"Does it have open seats?"

"Yes, there's a few seats left on it."

"I was able to get us two seats on my employee discount. They were only seventy-five bucks each. We're going to Nashville!"

Holy cannoli. I thought I was going to start to cry. I just looked back up at the clouds and mouthed *thank you*.

I believed it now. There were forces at work. I wasn't going to be intimidated by what was before us in Tennessee anymore. Now I was ready to learn.

WE PULLED UP TO Backyard Barbecue bright and early on a Monday morning after having a decent night's sleep in a Holiday Inn we would be staying at for the week. It looked much the way we expected, an old building, barn-like in appearance, mostly red and black with a lot of rough-hewn wooden trim. Hillbilly chic. We walked in, slightly surprised the front door was open so early in the morning. The dining room also held no surprises, looking roomy and casual. A lot of red checkered tablecloths, a lot of rustic wooden booths, and a long counter that ran along one end with a service window behind for the orders to be placed as they came up. A cash register was at one end.

No one seemed to be around. The front of the house was completely empty, though we could hear some noise in the back indicating people were back there. We didn't want to just barge in, so we waited a while, just checking out all we could see in the front.

I was excited. This was the real McCoy. I couldn't wait to see the place in action.

A young black woman in her twenties came out to the counter area from the back. She looked up at us in surprise.

"Hello!" I said. "We're looking for Gary."

"Oh, are you the folks coming in today? Gary's not here yet. He told me you were coming and for you to feel free to look at whatever you like. If you have any questions, we can try to answer them for you. I'm Venita. Pokey is messin' around in the back."

"When's Gary usually get here?"

"Well, that's anybody's guess. He usually gets here between ten and eleven."

It was 7:30.

"Gary's not here yet" or "Gary had to go out" or "Gary will be back later" was something we heard frequently that week. It was mostly up to us to explore, observe, and ask questions. We went into the back of the house, which was almost as large in area as the dining room. There was equipment, prep tables, stacks and stacks of boxes and canned goods along walls and under counters. It was overwhelming at first to take it all in.

Pokey, also black and looking to be in about his late twenties, was moving around, organizing things for the start of the day. We said hello and introduced ourselves. He nodded and told us to make ourselves at home.

"This is it." He gestured around the kitchen. "If y'all have any questions, just ask."

I didn't think my first question should be to ask what kind of questions I should be asking. I just tried to look like I was knowledgeably taking it all in, walking around acting like I was comparing everything to all the other barbecue places I had seen before. Yep, everything seemed in order. Now what?

Pokey just glanced at me and looked around. "Well, y'all wanna see the smokers?"

We followed him into a back room. Two large rotisserie smokers were side by side, set into a wall. Pokey opened one up to show several chunks of meat rotating around on racks, looking like they were close to being ready. We didn't say anything, so he pointed at one.

"This here's the pork butts," he said as a way of prompting us.

"Wow, how many are in there?"

"Oh, maybe a dozen, I guess. We cook more later in the week and on the weekend."

Then he opened the next one. "These are ribs and chicken." Again, the smoker was full of meat, freshly seasoned and at the beginning of its cooking cycle. It all looked mouthwatering and delicious to me. Leni was more just impressed with the scale of it all.

Pokey took us to a door leading outside. We could see the cabinet part of the smokers were out there, covered by a corrugated metal roof above them. Also protected from the weather was a huge stack of logs.

"What kind of wood is that?"

Pokey just gave me the look I would become quite used to that week from just about everyone who worked there. The look said, "Really?"

"It's hickory. You can use any ol' kind of fruit or nut wood, though."

"How long you cook the meats for?"

"Well, them porks go overnight, maybe ten to twelve hours. The chicken and ribs we cook in the morning, maybe four hours or so."

As we trailed Pokey around and watched Venita make sweet tea in two large commercial coffeemaking machines, other employees started coming in. Person after person would look at us, maybe be told who we were or not, give us a nod, and then continue on with their routine. Leni and I tried to stay out of their way and not look as stupid as we were feeling.

Finally, a white man in his mid-thirties came sweeping in. He was of medium height and build, had thinning brown hair and a mustache, and with a big smile introduced himself.

"Welcome, welcome, I'm Gary. How y'all doin'? Did you have a good trip? Did you get set up all right where you're stayin'? How's the place here lookin' to you? Are these knuckleheads treatin' you all right?"

He kept nodding at us between questions, our lack of immediate response seeming sufficient in moving rapidly along from one to the next. We assured Gary that Pokey and Venita had been very patient and helpful, and we were looking forward to seeing lunchtime in action.

"Y'all just make yourselves at home. Look at anything you like; ask whatever questions you may have. I'm just going upstairs to the office for a while. I have some product ordering I need to get done and some paperwork. There's always paperwork! Haw!"

I don't think we had seen and spoken to him for more than five minutes.

"Later on, I'll show you all the office work, the ordering and employee forms, record keeping, all that stuff. But, for now, you should probably just get a feel for how the food is handled. I think you'll have plenty to see with that for a while."

I couldn't argue with that.

"Gary? Gary?" Pokey was after him as he headed for the stairs to go to the office. "Can I see you a minute? What we was talkin' about?"

"Yes, Pokey, I know. Come up to the office. I'll take care of you." Gary rolled his eyes at me, kind of a "tell you later" look. Leni and I stood and looked after them as they went upstairs, not really knowing what to do next. We wandered through different areas, watching the employees work. Lunchtime came and we kept at a distance while they put out plate after plate of barbecue sandwiches, salads, and baked potatoes. We were really drawn by the salads and baked potatoes that were topped with smoked meats. I hadn't seen that before. We ended up trying those for lunch ourselves when Venita asked if we wanted something to eat.

The potatoes were slathered with butter, sour cream, shredded cheese, bacon bits, and green onions. Then they were topped with either pork, chicken, or turkey. The salads were in deep-fried flour taco shells with similar toppings and meat choices. We both were impressed. They were very tasty. Something I hadn't seen served in Seattle. Interesting.

We saw Gary again for a while in the afternoon. He walked us around showing us various pieces of equipment, how they were used, how they were maintained. Leni had brought a camera and I had her faithfully photographing everything. I wanted a complete visual record to rely on when we returned to Seattle.

Later on, Gary's sister Carla showed up. She looked close to Gary's age, about fifteen to twenty years younger than Leni and me, but I believe she was a little older than Gary. She was the manager for the evening crew; Gary was the manager during the day.

"Well, how y'all doin'? Welcome to our little ol' BBQ joint. Is Gary takin' care of you?"

"So far, so good. He stays pretty busy. We see him a little bit now and then."

"Oh, he's worthless. Are y'all stayin' close to here?"

"We're at the Holiday Inn."

"Oh, gracious. Well, I guess it'll have to do. But, I'm takin' y'all out tonight. You are our guests and tonight I want to take you to dinner. Have you eaten at Cracker Barrel before?"

"Uh, nope, can't say that we have."

"Well, you're in for a treat. We love our Cracker Barrel. I'm takin' y'all out. It's on me."

Carla was a sweetheart. Unfortunately, going out to dinner that night was the last time we ever saw her. We were never there in the evening after that.

 For the next two days we observed the whole process of how they set up in the morning, how they got their serving line ready, how they plated and served during lunchtime. We watched how they prepped, how they measured portions, how the orders were kept organized and expedited to go out properly. We were being completely schooled by a team of young people either fresh out of high school or not so freshly having dropped out of high school.

At some point Leni and I were encouraged to get our hands involved, to get on the serving line during lunch and put some plates out. This was a source of great amusement for the staff, as all the things they completely took for granted were unfamiliar and foreign to us. I was embarrassingly incompetent. I prided myself in the professionalism I brought to being a bartender and a restaurant manager at the Mayflower Park, but here among these people young enough to be my children, I wasn't able to even keep up. I had to be corrected and re-shown over and over. The same was true for Leni, but she wasn't taking it as seriously. This was more of a funny lark for her. For me it was sobering.

When we returned to our hotel after the second day, I was feeling depressed.

"I don't know, Leni, I'm getting overwhelmed. I can't keep up with the volume at lunchtime. I'm not really getting the hang of it. I don't know if I can do this."

"You're doing all right. You're just not used to it. It's all new. We still have a couple of days."

"I hope so. I guess I expected Gary to be working with us more. We just get him for short periods of time."

"There's not much he can do that we're not already getting from his workers. It'll be all right. I tell you what, tomorrow we're going to take a trip after lunch. There's a Confederate battlefield not too far away. Shiloh. I want to go see that. We could use a break, see something interesting."

"Yeah, OK. And Thursday we're going up to see Southern Pride."

"There you go—there's still lots of fun things coming up. Don't lose heart yet."

She was right. But I was finding that operating a barbecue restaurant involved a lot of hard work, and not a small amount of stress. The smokers, automated or not, had to be loaded and unloaded every day. They had to be cleaned and maintained on a regular basis. And there were many, many other tasks and duties that had to happen every single day to keep a restaurant operating efficiently and profitably. And, in addition to all of that, you better be keeping your customers happy, and your employees, and the health department. And you better hope nothing causes the general economy to go in the tank because eating out is one of the first things to get cut.

I wasn't sleeping so well in that Holiday Inn double bed.

Over the next two days, we got more involved with some serving, also being part of a team making two hundred pork sandwiches for an elementary school lunch catering order that came in during the morning and had to be delivered by noon. Gary had that place geared for volume orders and large group catering. That was why he had a large staff for both day and evening shifts. He showed me how to have cooked product refrigerated and frozen, so that it could be quickly taken out and prepped for large orders that suddenly came in.

He explained how to slip a cash advance to a worker who says they need some extra help, like Pokey did on the first morning we were there. Little things like that helped build employee loyalty. And he advised me on looking the other way sometimes when employees, usually teenagers, did immature things like seeing who could jump the furthest from a standing position on top of a prep table. Or having sword fights with broom handles. It helped keep the job fun for them. Unless, of course, somebody got hurt, which was bound to happen.

We did get out for some fun time. The summertime weather was great and Tennessee was beautiful. We drove to the Shiloh Civil War memorial area, admiring the scenic countryside and so many spacious homes on grassy lots that looked like they were half an acre in size. I put barbecue out of my mind for a while as I reflected on the terrible struggle that had occurred on the very grounds we were walking on a century earlier. The lives lost, men maimed and shattered, fighting for a cause each side was deeply committed to. My struggles to come to terms with feeling competent to work with barbecue were so insignificant in comparison. Yet nonetheless, my struggles they were.

We went out that night and found a bar where there was live country music being performed. A young man was singing and had a deep, rich voice that resonated such depth of feeling to his plaintive songs. He was good, but then, we were so close to Nashville, there was probably no shortage of talented country performers throughout the state. All of them looking for a way to break through, to live the dream they always imagined for themselves, to feel like they were doing what they were always meant to do.

I knew what that feeling was like. I knew how hard it was to achieve. How competitive, how subjective, how arbitrary and capricious it all was. What I was doing now wasn't the same as trying to be an actor, though it certainly had similarities. It was a long shot, a very long shot, and a deliberate step outside of my comfort zone. But it was the story I wanted for Leni and myself. Our story, our path for the time we were together. And even though I wasn't comfortable with it, it was happening. We were doing it.

And I could give her and myself at least a little credit for how far we had come, no matter how it turned out later on. Thinking about that let me relax and enjoy this powerful country singer's chops all the more.

THE SOUTHERN PRIDE MANUFACTURING warehouse was unassuming in appearance, looking much like any other industrial building. It was on the outskirts of Marion, Illinois, a small town that reminded me of many I had seen dotted around the central Texas area I grew up in. The only way we knew we found it was a blunt, block-lettered sign with the name on it. Underneath it was a smaller sign that said simply, "Office."

I was excited when the door opened and we walked inside to a large, unadorned room that had a reception counter close to the entrance and then linoleum floor space with several pieces of equipment haphazardly set apart on display. We arrived in the late afternoon, leaving Jackson after observing the morning and early lunch rush at Backyard Barbecue. I thought I gave enough time for the drive, but we ended up cutting it close, getting there less than an hour before closing.

I didn't need a lot of time. I just wanted to see the smoker, maybe talk to someone about it for a little while.

"Good afternoon," said the lady seated at a desk behind the reception counter.

I assumed she was the kind-sounding woman whom I had previously reached on the phone. I introduced Leni and myself and explained we were just there to see what the place looked like and to check out the smokers. It would be great if we could talk to someone about them a little bit.

She rose and went into a back office, so Leni and I wandered out onto the open floor. It didn't take long for me to come face to face with it, the Smoke Chef 200, the automated barbecue smoker that had captured me with its color photo in a restaurant industry magazine.

This was my moment of victory. I had arrived. The automated barbecue smoker that had been my quest, my obsession, was now before me. I had persevered through months of tentative, sometimes faltering, steps, but I made it to Marion, Illinois and was looking directly at the object of my imagined destiny.

A man came into the room, eyeing us warily. He looked to be only a few years older than me, lean, hard-edged, a face worn by a weathered ruggedness. He stopped a few feet from us, sizing me up critically.

"Hello," I said. "Are you able to tell us about the smokers?"

"I better be," he replied humorlessly. "I own the place."

"Oh, well, I'm honored."

"Everybody else has gone home. What is it you want to know?" This sullen-faced man was not one to suffer fools lightly, and I obviously fit the bill. After spending less than a minute showing us the SC 200, he asked if it was true, as his secretary had told him, that we had traveled from Seattle to see a smoker.

"We have a distributor out there. He probably has one or two of these in a warehouse. You could have looked at it out there. You could have put your hands on it, stuck your head in it, whatever you wanted. He's got brochures, spec sheets, all the information. There was really no need to come here."

I explained that we were down in Tennessee studying a restaurant I wanted to model mine after. If, that is, we could find a location for it. I just thought it would be fun to come up and look at where they were made. Gary's smokers were also Southern Prides, but I likely wouldn't be using ones that big. Not starting out anyway. He had a couple of the smaller SC 200s, but had stopped using them years ago and they were just sitting unceremoniously as dry storage cabinets.

"Uh-huh." He had no interest in my journey, my story, or in spending any more time with me than he had to. He had people he paid for that. "Anything else I can do for you? We're gettin' ready to close."

Driving back to Jackson, I ruminated on my inauspicious reception at Southern Pride and the generally rocky week I was having at Backyard Barbecue.

"Am I biting off more than I can chew, Leni? Am I trying too hard to make this all work?"

"I think you've done an amazing job of it. I can't believe we're really here."

"It's all a lot harder than I thought it would be."

"Oh, everything is, honey. Life is hard. You have to give yourself some time. Everything we're seeing, everything we're doing, it's all brand new. Wait until we get back to Seattle. I think when we're home and you can relax and not feel the pressure of being here, you'll realize you've learned a lot."

"Yeah, maybe."

"But it's up to you, darling. I'm just along for the ride. And, so far, it's been a pretty nice ride."

She looked out the window and I felt, not for the first time, how grateful and how lucky I was to have her with me.

ON OUR FINAL DAY at Backyard Barbecue I didn't try to get on the serving line anymore. There wasn't anything more to prove. I understood how they operated, I knew the menu intimately, I had watched every step of the morning prep routine. I wasn't good enough to work on the line, but I was good enough to hire my own young people and show them how I wanted it done.

I knew how to set up my kitchen and my serving counter. I knew what kind of equipment was needed. I knew how to season and cook the meats. I knew how to operate and maintain the smokers. There was actually quite a lot that I knew now, more than the vast majority of people in Seattle did.

Gary took us into his office and we spent time talking about catering and all the business side of operating a restaurant. He gave me lots of employee forms and some of his lists for inventory and product ordering. He showed me profit and loss statements and explained the different line items, how the percentages should come out to stay above break-even.

When we reached the point where I didn't have any more questions for him, it was time to settle up. Actually, I was supposed to have done that the first day we arrived, but he had waved it off and said we could handle it later. Now as I made out the check, I asked, "I already sent the deposit, so the total for both of us is three thousand, right?"

Gary, sitting across from me behind his desk, rubbed his chin. "Well, I haven't been around for y'all this week as much as I should have been, probably. You've had to fend for yourselves a lot. Why don't we just call it twenty-five hundred?"

I thanked him for that. If I was able to keep going, I might need every dollar I had. I felt Gary had delivered everything he promised. I had seen and experienced a real barbecue restaurant up close and personally. I knew what I was getting myself into. I handed him my check in full satisfaction that I had gotten my money's worth.

CHAPTER TWENTY-ONE

ON SATURDAY, BACK IN Seattle, I called Robert Sindelar.

"No, sorry, still don't have anything new. Nothing different from what I told you before."

"Well, I'll try you again next week."

"That'll be fine."

When I got off the phone, Leni was indignant. We had talked about it on the plane coming back and agreed that Lake Forest Park would be an ideal place to start in. It was less intimidating and risky than trying to start with Pete's place or some other freestanding restaurant. And besides those two locations, there really wasn't anyplace else emerging as a realistic possibility for us.

"Why is he jerking you around like that? Is the space rented or not? We need to know so we can make our own decisions. He needs to make up his mind if he is going to take you seriously or not."

"Well, I'm sure he's waiting for Jones Barbecue to commit. That's who they really want."

"To hell with them. We're ready to go. Tell him if they won't commit, we will. If he keeps messing around he's going to lose them and us. Does he want that space rented or not?"

"I guess that means you're ready to do this."

"I don't care one way or the other. But I don't like him screwing around with you like that. He needs to get off the fence. You should tell him that."

"I'll try to press him harder the next time I talk to him. I promise."

The next day I took Leni to Magnuson Park at Sand Point for something I had seen an article about in *The Seattle Post-Intelligencer* a couple of weeks earlier. It was the Low & Slow Pro BBQ State Championship. I had to see it. The article stated there would be professional pit masters there from Alabama and Florida. Enthusiasts could attend between 9 a.m. and 4 p.m. and watch the teams preparing entries, ask questions about techniques, and check out the different barbecue pits. Prominent local chefs were going to be there, as well.

I walked all around the different booths, tasting ribs or anything else there was available. There was a big crowd there, and hundreds of people either competing in the cook-off or promoting their businesses from catering to barbecue sauces, from grills to cookbooks, from any and all sorts of things related to barbecue.

Seeing the turnout for this event drove it home to me again that my idea for a barbecue restaurant in this area was spot-on. It was obvious there was a big demand. I had never before heard of a BBQ State Championship in Washington State. Maybe there was one, but it was never on my radar. I was convinced that I was going to start seeing barbecue restaurants popping up in the north end. If I didn't do it, someone else would. And I would just be watching it happen and kicking myself for having worked so hard and come so close just to let it slip from my grasp in the end.

"Come on, Leni, let's go over to Lake Forest Park. I want to look at that Al's Diner space again."

When we went in, we saw people setting up lots of folding chairs in The Commons area facing the stage. It looked like they were getting ready for something they were expecting a crowd for later.

The Al's Diner space was still dark, still as we had first seen it with Tom in July. I stood looking into it, imagining how it could work for a barbecue restaurant. I could see it, where two SC 200s could fit under the grill exhaust hood. There was already a char broiler and a deep fryer that I could put to use. I saw where I could put a hot hold cabinet, a bun rack.

I could see where the serving line would be, just like it was set up at Backyard Barbecue. They had two stations there. This only had room for one, but it would be enough. I wouldn't be doing anywhere near the volume they had in the beginning. I could see in the back how I could set up all my prep stations; the refrigerators and freezer were already there. The three-sink for dish washing; the hand sinks for sanitation. I could see it. It was all there, or could be there so easily.

"Is that him?"

Leni had spotted Robert. I had described him to her when I told her about meeting with him. He was walking briskly, looking like he was preoccupied with something important. He glanced over and saw us.

"Oh, hello." He stopped briefly.

I introduced Leni and said we were just looking at the space again. We just got back from Tennessee, where we were studying a restaurant there, and we were comparing how this space could translate into what we wanted to do.

"Oh, uh-huh, sure, look as much as you want."

"We didn't expect to see you. I didn't know you work on Sunday."

"I don't. We just have this author event going on. I'm usually not here on Sunday."

"You must be busy. It looks like there's going to be a lot of people. We'll let you get to it."

"Thanks, I'll talk to you soon." He started to walk away.

Leni said, "Just a minute. Robert?"

He turned. "Yes?"

"I think you need to know something."

He looked quickly at me and then back to her. "Yes?"

"We want to lease this space. We have an idea that would work really well here. We've worked hard on it. But we can't just keep sitting around waiting. We need a decision on whether you will lease this space to us or not. We need to know one way or the other."

Then she stared him down.

"Right. You're right. This is taking too long." He turned to me. "I'll call Ron tomorrow. Give me a call in the afternoon. I'll try to tell you something more definite then. OK?"

I had been holding my breath. I finally let it go. "Yes, thank you. I'll call you tomorrow."

"Great. Well, I really have to get to this."

"Sure, thanks again." And he hustled away.

I looked at Leni and she gave me a curt nod. "That's how you do it."

Not bad for somebody who said she didn't care one way or the other.

ON MONDAY MORNING I was at my desk in the basement of the Mayflower Park Hotel. Steve J. was off after having worked the weekend as the manager on duty, a rotating obligation shared by upper management. I had just settled in when the phone rang. It was Angie, the executive secretary, telling me Mr. Ishii would like to see me in his office.

My heart sank. He knew. I couldn't be sure who he got it from, but Steve J. was my primary suspect. The two of them were close and Steve probably was uncomfortable not being completely forthcoming with him.

"I'll be right up."

I stopped in the hallway to pull my suit jacket from a rack and slip it on. I checked myself in a mirror and straightened my tie. This was the first time in all the years at the hotel I was being called into the general manager's office for something I could be in trouble for. I took a deep breath and walked to the elevator.

"Hi! How was your vacation?" Angie gave me a big smile like she always did. "He's ready for you. Go right in."

I wasn't sure I was ready for him.

Paul Ishii was as decent and kind as any man I've ever known. When he made me a manager for the first time, he sent me down to Nordstrom's to be fitted for a dark business suit on the hotel's account. He took Steve J. and me to a furniture warehouse to pick out a pair of desks that would fit across from each other in the office we were to share from that time forward. I really did not want to see him look disappointed in me.

"So... I understand you've been on an adventure, laying the groundwork for leaving us."

This was painful, but I had to own it. Paul listened patiently while I shared as much of the story as I could without drawing it out too long. I assured him I wasn't letting this outside interest interfere with any aspect of my duties and responsibilities to the hotel, and that I wouldn't take any action without knowing I could give him more than ample notice.

He nodded and spoke softly. "You know, you are very highly thought of around here. By your co-workers and the customers. And by the Dempseys. You're considered family to those who have known you around here for so many years."

"I can appreciate that. I tell you, Paul, this has all surprised me somewhat that I've gone as far as I have with it. It's a huge risk. And I know how lucky I am to be here, to have the job here that I do. I don't know if I can explain it very well, but I just feel like this might be the last chance I have to do something that's truly my own. I want to play this out until it either happens or else I realize it just won't."

"You haven't made any decisions yet?"

"I don't know if Steve mentioned it, but I'm taking one more trip. This weekend I'm going down to Texas. My family gets together in vacation timeshares on the beach at South Padre Island. I'm hoping to get some input from them. I should know after that what I really want to do."

"I tell you what, you go down there and do what you need to do, take the time you need to figure it out. But before you make a decision, talk with me one more time. I just want a final chance to try and change your mind. Can you give me that?"

"Of course I can."

From the first time I laid eyes on that picture of an automated barbecue smoker, I had experienced a myriad of feelings during each step in the journey. Inspiration, excitement, hope, rejuvenation, fear, despair, defeat, and a host of others from positive to negative. This was the first time my feeling was sorrow, and maybe a little shame.

That afternoon I called Robert Sindelar as he had requested me to. He got on the phone and, as usual, did not beat around the bush.

"Ron would like to meet you. Can you have a meeting here with him on Wednesday morning before going into your job?"

Most definitely I could. The Al's Diner space was not a lock for Jones Barbecue. I had a foot in the door. I had all the ammunition I needed and a little time to get ready.

After the meeting I had with Paul, there was more of a calmness within me. I had a great job already. Even if I did not open a barbecue restaurant, the world would not come to an end. I was in a place where I was appreciated and wanted. It was actually getting kind of tough to walk away from it.

But that Al's Diner space was perfect for us. And I was just back from learning so much in Tennessee. And we had already come so far. It was feeling like destiny.

CHAPTER TWENTY-TWO

ON TUESDAY STEVE J was back, and he grilled me on the trip to Tennessee.

"What was the BBQ guy like? How was the kitchen set up? What was the food like?

I couldn't give him enough details.

"Steve, I have a meeting in the morning with the man who owns the space at Lake Forest Park we've been looking at. It's important in determining if we will go in there or not. I might be a little late getting in."

"No problem, I got you covered. Are you ready for it?"

"I think so. I've done everything I can think of up to this point. I'll give it my best shot."

Susil was in to ask how my plans were going and how much I would be looking for in investment. Was I ready to show him my location?

"Not yet, Susil. Still working out some details. I'll let you know something soon."

"I want to eat some of the food. I've been learning about it. I want to taste what you will be serving."

"I understand. I'll get back to you when I get some things set up."

I wasn't sure how far I wanted to go with Susil. For now, I needed to hold him off. The idea of him was a good backup plan, but I wanted to stay independent if I could.

Everywhere in the hotel I was getting peppered with questions and comments about starting my own barbecue restaurant. What I was doing was generally common knowledge now. If I backed down, I would have to suffer a long period of explaining why I didn't go through with it. The suspense was building. Would I really do it? Or was it all just a bunch of talk?

That night I went over my business plan, my projected menu, a personal resume. I organized the pictures of equipment we had taken at Backyard Barbecue, and I had lists of them and a couple of floor plans Jeff Winter had made up, some material that would show Ron Sher I had a professional general contractor working with me.

There was nothing left to organize. Leni and I just needed to get a good night's sleep. We were both so charged up, that proved to be a challenge.

"GOOD MORNING, I'M RON Sher."

He stood up and greeted Leni and me warmly. Robert had met us when we came into the bookstore and brought us out to where Ron was already sitting at a long wooden table in the middle of The Commons. It was very close to the same spot I had made my first pitch to Robert about three or four weeks earlier.

Ron was a tall man. I'm taller than most people I meet, but he stood a little above me. He had a tanned, creased face with a neatly trimmed beard that framed it. Although he looked to be nearing seventy, he was lean and energetic, a man who lived vigorously both with his body and mind.

I dove right in to my presentation, looking him steadily in the eye with complete conviction. Six months' worth of work poured out of me. From the first faltering meeting with Ed Molzan, through all of the stops and starts along the way, capped with a week in Tennessee and a final handshake with Gary Christian, everything had contributed toward preparing me to meet this singular opportunity. I had studied the Al's Diner space and knew, after having Backyard Barbecue practically memorized, exactly what I wanted to do with it.

Ron listened approvingly as I went over the business plan and showed him pictures of equipment. He nodded in agreement as I showed him the menu I intended to serve and told him of the lack of any competition in the area. He didn't need any more convincing. He gazed at the Al's Diner space for a moment, narrowing his eyes and thinking deeply. Then he said, mostly for Robert's benefit, "What we need is to completely erase the memory of Al's Diner. People should never be reminded in any way of what was there before."

Robert said, "You don't want to wait until the end of the month for..."

"No, no, we've waited long enough. We're ready to go here."

He looked back at me. "We've got some woodworking artists with a workshop in Ballard who have done some beautiful work for us in the past. They made this table, several of these tables. They like to reclaim fallen old-growth timber, a lot of it is shipped down from Alaska. Robert, why don't you give Richard a call and see how his schedule looks?"

I was trying to keep up. "I...uh...I..."

"It's clear that your focus is on your concept. You know what you want to do and how you want to do it. My strong point is branding and merchandising, making it look right. Do you know what you want to call it?"

I didn't have a clue what I was going to call it, but I didn't want to tell him that.

"I'm kicking around a couple of names. We're going down to Texas this weekend for a family gathering. I was planning to finalize it with them."

"Well, we can take care of all of the facade work. What do you think, Robert, about twelve thousand for a TI budget?"

"Yes, we could do that," he replied.

Ron kept steamrolling ahead. "We'll give you a five-year lease with a three-year option. That's pretty standard. The tenant improvement budget will be figured into the lease. We'll recoup that over time."

I said, "Sure, sure." He was giving me money?

"There's not too much to do on the interior. You have a lot of equipment in there you can use, right?"

"Yes, I do."

"We won't charge you anything for that. I understand you're just starting out. We'll give you three months without rent for the build-in. If you can open before that, that's some extra money to get you going. If there are problems with opening in time, we can address that when we know what they are." He looked at Robert again. "Does that cover everything?"

Robert nodded briskly. "That should be good for now."

Ron smiled, turned back to me, and said, "Do we have a deal?"

I blurted out, "Yes sir, we have a deal."

"Good. Robert will draw up a letter of intent for the two of you to sign. You can give him a check for the security deposit and first month's rent, and we'll be set. After that, I'll have our legal team draw up the lease. Congratulations, I'm looking forward to working with you both."

We shook hands one last time and that was it. We were in. I had an agreement to open a barbecue restaurant. And in that instant, I knew what I wanted to call it.

Leni and I walked out of the Lake Forest Park Town Center in shock.

"Oh my God," she kept saying, "What just happened? Are we really doing this?"

"Well, that's what we need to decide."

"Didn't you just tell him we are?"

"Yes, I did, but we haven't signed anything yet. It's not a binding agreement until we put it in writing and give them some money."

"I'm confused. Aren't you happy about this? Isn't this what you wanted?"

"It's exactly what I wanted. I just wasn't ready for it to happen the first time I met the man. I thought he would want some time to think about it, to consider if he wanted us or Jones Barbecue. I didn't think he would just rent it to us like that."

Leni looked hard at me. "Are you scared? Are you having second thoughts?"

"No, Leni, I'm not having second thoughts. I gave my word to Paul Ishii I wouldn't make a final decision without talking to him about it one last time. I'm feeling like I'm not keeping my word. But, I couldn't say that to Ron Sher. I didn't want to blow the whole deal."

"So, you'll tell Paul Ishii you're going to do it?"

"It looks like I will. But, it's not official yet. I could still change my mind. I have to hear what he has to say. It's possible I could decide to stay at the hotel."

Then we looked at each other and broke out giggling.

CHAPTER TWENTY-THREE

NOW I WAS IN it. I had what I wanted. All I had to do was sign a piece of paper and hand over a check. I thought I should have been ecstatically happy, and on one level I was. I couldn't wait to start making calls. To Lynne, telling her to put the house on the market and get out there and beat the streets to find us a cheap condo. To Daniel Petzoldt, telling him things were in motion and I would be in soon to arrange for everything we had discussed to become real. To Jeff Winter, saying I had nailed the location, thanks to him, and we were a go to plan it out and execute. To John Head, telling him I needed him to plan on a return trip to help me with employee training and to finalize cooking schedules. And finally, to Ed Molzan, saying I wanted to set up another meeting to go over where I was and what I should do next. I wanted to wait and tell him about getting a location in person. I wanted to see his face.

This was my victory lap. My "I told you so" moment; *I told you I could do this.* It wasn't just telling people I had an idea anymore. Now it was real.

On another level, I was surprised to find it unsettling, at times disturbing. For one thing, I had to say goodbye to a lot of people I liked and respected at the Mayflower Park Hotel. Some of them had worked closely with me for many years. There was no one at the hotel I was uncomfortable with and glad to be leaving. After seventeen years, it was like I was leaving home to go to college.

That was the other reason it troubled me. Just like a young man venturing onto a college campus where nothing was familiar anymore—none of his teachers, none of his classmates—I was equally pushing off into the unknown. I had to build new relationships with Ron Sher, Robert Sindelar, and a number of people who worked in the Lake Forest Park Town Center and Third Place Books. I'd have to win over the people who came into and frequented The Commons. I'd have to prove myself.

Could I do that? Had I seen and learned enough in Tennessee to make a real restaurant from it? Would the right people show up for me to hire who were critical for the actual day-to-day operation?

It was clear that even though I could take pleasure in getting a location, what I thought was a great location, I was still far from out of the woods. In fact, this was the point where my mettle and my commitment to what I was doing would really be tested.

Which feelings were going to take control inside me, my faith and confidence or my fear and insecurity? There were still miles to go before this journey was done.

PAUL AND I LEFT the hotel and walked a couple of blocks to the Icon Grill. We requested and were seated in a booth, allowing us a sense of privacy from the lunchtime diners around us. On the walk over and while considering our menus the conversation had been kept light, innocuous. Neither of us seemed to want to be aggressive. I think both of us knew how this would go.

I had already had a conversation with Steve J., telling him that I had a location and it was just a matter of pulling the trigger. He acted like it wasn't that surprising to him; he wished he could make a similar move. He understood my desire for wanting to strike out on my own, to not always be a good steward taking care of the Dempseys' business.

"You're going to do great," he said. "You're going to be doing it for yourself and it will mean so much more to you for it."

I had to let down Susil, but I tried not to close that door completely.

"I lucked into a fantastic situation, Susil. The space is already, for the most part, built out as I need it. I'm just going to have to equip it to my specifications, and put in menu boards and signs. It's going to cost a fraction of what I had expected to start it. I think I can do it on my own."

"Well, good for you. That's best. You don't have to satisfy anyone else. No one else has to be involved."

"If this business is successful, I hope to open more than one. I'd like to be able to come to you in the future if the circumstances are right for it."

"Of course! I'll be here. Come talk to me anytime."

I had started informing my closest friends there and could sense both enthusiasm for wanting me to succeed and poignancy for me not being there anymore. The last step was the lunch with Paul. It was still possible for me to pull a reversal, but highly unlikely. My mind was already made up.

After placing our orders and receiving some iced tea, Paul finally addressed the subject head-on.

"Is there something that would make the job more meaningful to you? Can we give you a title, like Associate Food and Beverage Manager? Are there new areas you would like to be more involved in, Catering or Room Service? Would you like to be more involved in the restaurant again?"

"I'm not really looking for that, Paul. I'm very happy with the job of overseeing Oliver's."

"Would you like to go back to school? We could offer tuition assistance if you wanted to work toward an advanced degree."

"I'm almost fifty years old, Paul."

"We could give you a raise. Ten percent? Maybe some incentive bonuses in addition to shoot for."

"I've always felt I've been paid very generously for what I do around the hotel. I'm very appreciative of everything you've done for me over the years."

"I know you are. That's why it's so hard to see you leave."

We went through our lunch, talking about different memories we had of the Martini Challenge, of encounters with Mrs. Dempsey, of the parade of characters that Oliver's seemed to always attract. At the end he insisted on picking up the check, and then we were on the street heading back to the hotel.

"Is there any way we can support you in making the transition?"

"It's going to be two to three months before I get to opening. It would help a lot if I could keep coming to work for five or six weeks while we ramp up. I could use the paychecks."

"No problem. Take as long as you need."

We walked in silence for a moment, turning the corner. The hotel was just up ahead.

"Do you need an ice machine?"

"An ice machine? I haven't thought about it yet."

"We have one on the sixth floor that is making too much noise. We're going to have to replace it. It works, though. It would save you three or four thousand from having to buy a new one. You just have to arrange to have it hauled out."

"Sure, I can use that. I'll look into it. Thanks."

"Save money wherever you can. As a small business owner, you'll learn that fast."

I met with Robert Sindelar at the end of the week to pick up the letter of intent. It was only two typed pages. I told him I would have it back after Leni and I returned from our quick trip to Texas.

"Don't sit on it too long," he said seriously, "We want it signed before we can generate a lease.

That takes some time and also costs us some money. We were hoping to have everything in place at the beginning of September."

His look was saying, "Are you getting cold feet, rookie?"

"I'll have it back to you early next week. Leni has to sign it, too. I want to give her a chance to read it over because she has to be in this with me one hundred percent."

"Well, there's no surprises in it. It's everything we discussed and agreed on in the meeting. Are you having any different thoughts or considerations? Anything you see as a problem?"

After the lunch meeting with Paul, I was having more thoughts and considerations than I ever wanted Robert Sindelar to know about. I was leaving a job where I was safe and secure. I was offered almost anything I wanted to remain there.

Instead, I was about to sail off into a vast unknown ocean of possibilities. I didn't have a crew yet, wasn't sure if that crew would help me sail to the promised land or sink us along the way. I wasn't sure how seaworthy my vessel was. It might weather the storms or it might break apart in the first rough seas. And the captain was untested. Worse than that, inexperienced. He only had a Tennessee treasure map he kept studying and believing in to navigate forward with. Yes, I had deep considerations.

"Robert, this ship is ready to sail. I'll see you first thing when I get back next week."

When I told people we had found our location, the one person whom I hadn't yet reached out to was the one at the top of the list. My brother. Actually, he had found the location. He was the one to lead Leni and me up the escalator into Third Place Books. I knew I wasn't able to do it without him, and it had been true from the very beginning.

I was about to see him at South Padre, though, so I wanted to wait until then. I figured he had passed on the experience of coming to Seattle to look at the barbecue business with me. At least to my sister, Gerry, anyway. I wanted to break it to all the family members who were at South Padre at the same time, giving them the rundown on all we had learned in Tennessee, and then triumphantly proclaim our first location was locked up and we were on our way.

My hope was to get them caught up in the amazing, almost Divinely guided, progress I had made from a bizarre, half-baked idea to anticipated successful fruition. I had plans for these people. They were part of my overall strategy.

At the top of the list was my brother, Tom. The ball started rolling because of him. I wanted him to take care of the whole financial side of the business. I needed him to partner with me, or at least work closely with me until I made it successful enough that he would be drawn into partnering with me. He was primary to my plans.

Next was my sister, Gerry. I had learned a lot from studying Gary's menu items at Backyard Barbecue, and I was planning to ask for plenty of input from John Head on the meats, but I really wanted Gerry to come be with us when we settled on the recipes for all the side dishes and desserts. She was great in the kitchen, always the magnet for drawing the family together for holidays throughout the years, pleasing everyone with a feast of delicious home-cooking. I knew she could help me develop an authentic southern style for our sides and desserts.

Then there was her daughter, Stacy, and husband, Joel, the MIT grads. Those two understood technology and they understood business. They were relatively young, out of college for less than five years, but they were already wowing us with their rapid accent in pioneering dot-coms and finding opportunities to write their own ticket for career advancement pretty much in any technology company they thought might interest them. I wanted Stacy to help me with making a brand, a logo, something that would be the look of everything that my business projected to the public. For now, just having their enthusiasm and input would be very satisfying.

South Padre Island is a very pleasant place. The surf is usually warm and not too rough. The beach is soft sand, easy to dig your toes into. There's plenty of room for lots of people to spread out with umbrellas and beach blankets. The temperatures can get hot—it is Texas after all—but it's usually much cooler at the beach than it is inland. As long as a hurricane doesn't crash the party, it's a fine place to relax and vacation in.

When Leni and I arrived, this was going to be a quick trip, so I didn't bring kids with me. I was greeted with customary affection, as befitted the relative least commonly seen and least understood of all who were gathered to vacation together. Nothing of any import was immediately brought out. The order of the day was beach time, a nice cabana lunch somewhere, a quick trip into Mexico to haggle at a marketplace for blankets and jewelry, and then margaritas and nachos in a festive, authentic cantina.

I had a couple of probing questions about my "barbecue restaurant idea," but I put them off with a promise to reveal all before too long. I didn't want to seem like I was there to be a salesman, like I was trying to give them an infomercial recruiting them for my grand new scheme. I waited as long as I could until I thought the timing was right.

In the evening of the third day that we were there (we were leaving the next day), everyone was assembled to play card games and eat pizza. I announced that it was time for me to reveal some news. The room became quiet as they awaited my pronouncement.

"Well, I think most of you already know that Leni and I have been to Tennessee, and we've been studying a barbecue restaurant there."

I gave a concise rundown of as much as I could, including our jaunt into Illinois to visit Southern Pride.

"When we returned to Seattle, we were able to lock in a location." I looked at Tom. "It's in a shopping-mall type of place with a food court. That's where we're going to start."

Tom said, "That bookstore we went into?"

"Yes! They've agreed to rent us the space we saw that day."

He just nodded his head with tight lips. Not the reaction I was hoping for. Stacy took the lead.

"You know, the profit margin in restaurants are typically not very good. It's a tough business to make money in."

"I asked Charlotte at Ironworks BBQ in Austin after I heard what you were doin'." This was Mike, Gerry's husband. "They got the best barbecue in Austin. I been knowin' Charlotte for years. Their barbecue sauce has won national awards. They ship it all over the country. It's not my favorite sauce, though. I go there for the brisket. And the beef ribs. Those are the best in Austin."

"Dad?" Stacy prodded. "Can you get to the point, please?"

"Charlotte said, 'Tell him it's a lot of work.' That's what she said. 'It's a lot of work.' She would know. That place goes gangbusters every day. She's been doin' it for over twenty-five years. They're the best in Austin."

"Don't you remember what it was like with our dad when he had that drive-in?" My sister was weighing in. "You were probably too little to remember it much—he was gone all the time. I never saw him. He always had to be working. He had no time for being with his family. I hated that."

This was not turning into the celebratory embrace I had imagined and hoped for it to be. This was an intervention. They were all grouped across the room from me, tag-teaming in playing devil's advocate to my grand intentions.

"I just don't want to see that happen to you," she went on. "Operating a small business can make it very difficult to make time for being with Hannah and Kyle and Echo."

I countered that I wasn't really spending all that much time with them now anyway. They were often more preoccupied being with their friends. I thought I might have a chance to have all three of them work with me in the business, give them teenage jobs. It might actually bring us closer together and allow us to spend more time together than we were before.

Tom's daughter, Amy, said, "I think that could be scary, working for your dad. I mean, as a teenager. It could be a little intimidating."

I could see the writing on the wall. They all thought I was being impetuous again, going off half-cocked into something completely irrational. And they were right. But they hadn't walked in my shoes. They hadn't seen and done what I had in the last six months.

Gerry's son, Ryan, asked, "Have you come up with a name for it yet?"

"As a matter of fact, I think I have. I'd like to call it Burney Brothers BBQ."

Tom laughed. "Really? Why?"

"Because you basically found it for us that day. And I would really like your help with it—with the financial statements, the accounting, the planning—to work together and see if we can make it grow."

"Well, I can certainly do that."

"I even thought up a motto: 'Burney Brothers BBQ. It's purty—spelled p-u-r-t-y—dang good.'"

Groans all around.

"Look, y'all, I've been a good soldier for the Mayflower Park Hotel for almost seventeen years. I've never worked another job even close to that long. In my whole life, all my other jobs combined wouldn't be as long. I don't think I'll ever find another job as good. I believe, if I pass up this opportunity to do something on my own, I'll keep working at the Mayflower until I retire. That wouldn't be so bad. I could do a lot worse."

I paused to see if they were with me. The looks I saw were empathetic, caring.

"But I'd rather not just take care of the hotel's bar for the rest of my working life. I'd really like to test myself one more time. I'd really like to see if I can make a business work and be successful. And I believe a barbecue place in the area of Seattle I'm in would work very well."

There was a silence in the room, and then Leni spoke. "I think I feel the same way about flying. I don't really want to do it forever."

Tom said, "We're not trying to talk y'all out of it. We just want you to really think about what you're doing. It's very risky. And a lot of times things we build up in our head don't really come out the way we imagined in the harsh light of reality."

"I'll take responsibility for what I'm doing. I think I've always done that. And I'll do it this time as well. I'm prepared to give everything I've got to making this work."

"That's what I'm afraid of," Gerry said. "You'll be working all the time and we'll never see you again."

The next day Leni and I had to leave them, but before we went, I got assurances from each and every one that they absolutely wished me the best and were excited to hear news of how it was going later on. Stacy told me she had a good friend who was a talented graphic artist. She was sure her friend could design a logo I would be happy with. Gerry said if I wanted her to make the trip to Seattle to help with finalizing the menu items, then she would definitely come for me. Tom said he would be there, too, to get my cash register set up and all my daily bookkeeping in place. I could send everything to him monthly for reconciliation and he would send back profit and loss statements, just like he had done for the RV park over the years we were managing it.

At the end of it all, when we were on a plane heading back to Seattle, I received pretty much what I had been hoping to get in contributions from my family members. Stacy was going to help me in the way I knew she could, and Tom and Gerry were going to come help me get the restaurant opened when the time came. But none of them in Texas wanted anything to do with it after that. And I couldn't blame them.

This was going to be all Leni and me. Our story, our path. For now, anyway. Maybe I could change some minds over time if we became successful. But I would have to prove it first.

Back in Seattle, I sat in the comfortable evening air on the back patio of our house in Shoreline. Lynne had been by to go over some things we should do in preparation for putting the house on the market. Her and Leni made a plan for going out to look at condos later in the week.

I had the letter of intent in my hands. I didn't need to read it anymore. It wasn't about what was on paper. This was the moment of truth. The point of no return.

I had told Ron Sher and Robert Sindelar we had a deal. I had told Paul Ishii there was nothing new, that the location was a lock. I had told my family that everything was set for me to open my own barbecue restaurant.

Now I just needed to sign the paper. It wasn't really official, of course. That would be the lease. That weighty document was still to come. However, I knew I wouldn't renege on signing the lease.

This was my last chance to reverse myself. It would be embarrassing. I would eat crow for a long time with just about everyone I knew. But I wouldn't have done any harm to myself or anyone else. All of the stuff I had been feeling and expressing to others about wanting to break away and do something of my own, to have Leni and me write our own story, to have a final try at creating a successful business with an idea I really believed in, all of that stuff, was it real? Did I believe it? Was I willing to bet everything I had on it? I talked a big game, but was I really ready to back it up and do whatever it took to make it happen?

I wrote my name on the paper as big as John Hancock, and I took it inside to let Leni do the same. Burney Brothers BBQ was born.

PART THREE

The Outcome

The Reality vs. The Idea
2004–2019

CHAPTER TWENTY-FOUR
September 2004

JEFF WINTER MET LENI and me at the Town Center to take a walk-through of our new restaurant. We pushed open the swinging metal door, letting us inside the kitchen, and flipped on the lights for the first time.

Wow. I was still wrapping my mind around it. Our new restaurant. I had a whole new agenda. Conception stage was over. Implementation stage had begun.

Ron Sher was giving me three rent-free months to open. That would put us at the beginning of December. I wanted to beat that. I asked Jeff if we could have everything delivered and installed by early November.

"I don't see any reason why not," he asserted confidently. "Everything is already here, even the hood. We'll probably need to have some electrical work done to accommodate the smokers, but most of the rest seems pretty well set."

As I watched Jeff take measurements, Leni wandered all through the space with her arms crossed, tightly gripping her elbows.

"Oh! It's filthy!" She kept looking at me, shaking her head and grimacing. "It's disgusting! Did they ever clean in here?"

"Well, it's been closed for a few months," I offered.

"There's grease and dust everywhere. Even the walls are caked with it. We have to clean this up. This is unacceptable." She kept finding new areas to shudder at. I kept my attention on Jeff.

"The hotel offered me a big ice machine. I think it could fit in the corner by the door, but it's really huge. I'll pay you guys to go get it."

"Sure. That would be a lot cheaper than buying a new one."

"Yeah, that's what I'm thinking, and while we're on that subject…" Paul's advice to save money wherever I could resonated inside me. "Before you order all the equipment, I'd just like to have a last look at the used stuff that's in a couple of those secondhand restaurant equipment stores down in the industrial district in SODO. I doubt I'll find anything, but I'd like to give it one more try."

"I'll need four to six weeks to get everything shipped in. Sometimes it can take longer if there's unforeseen delays in transit. You don't want to cut it too close."

"I'll confirm with you by next week. I just want to see what's out there that I might be able to use."

The month of September flew by. There was not a day we weren't on the go from the time we got out of bed until well into the evening.

I stayed diligent with my duties at the hotel. I didn't want anyone insinuating I was any kind of a short-timer, letting things slide, and coasting through the days to just collect my paychecks. I was talking a lot about my impending departure, though. Everyone wanted to know about my barbecue restaurant plans.

With whatever free time I had after work and on weekends, I was busy lining up the vendors and services I would need to get my restaurant to opening: a sign company to make menu boards, a printing press company for menus, business cards, and fliers. I met with the two guys from Ballard who Ron Sher had set me up with for putting up all of the restaurant facade. I met with insurance guys. I went to the health department. I talked to food service vendors and meat companies and soda pop dispenser reps. I went to every secondhand restaurant equipment store I could find, coming up empty at all of them. I was about to throw in the towel with that idea, but then I considered one more store that I saw in the yellow pages. It required a drive over to Tacoma and I thought it was likely a waste of time, but Leni and I were up for an afternoon drive, so we went over there on a lark.

I was completely unfamiliar with Tacoma, the smelly smaller sibling to Seattle, so we spent a good while being lost until finally stumbling onto it, a sprawling industrial district warehouse operated by a man named Massoud. He had a mumbling, almost indecipherable accent. Was it Afghan? Syrian? Iraqi? I had no clue.

His store, if it could be called that, was giant. Rooms and rooms with every kind of restaurant service equipment, shoved together and stacked up on shelves along the wall. It seemed like finding anything specific would be impossible.

I started showing him pictures we had taken in Tennessee of the different things I needed.

"Oh yes!" he proclaimed, and went straight to what I was looking for. He had a Cres Cor hot hold cabinet, the exact model I wanted. It was one-third the price of buying it new. He showed me the exact hot holding two-drawer unit I wanted for holding my meats on the serving line while we were plating them. Again, a fraction of what it would cost me new.

I could have even gotten a smoker from him, a Southern Pride, but I had assured Jeff that I wanted my two smokers to be brand new. They were going to be my workhorses. After all the work Jeff had done for me, so far for nothing, I didn't want to cut too much of my business away from him.

I got a couple of stainless prep tables, some pots and five-pound scales. Massoud even threw in a two-pound scale with a cracked plastic face that we could use on the line for portioning as a gift.

Our little jaunt over to Tacoma ended up saving me about four thousand dollars.

Lynne came through like a champ. She had been showing our house to prospective buyers and also going out with Leni day after day to look at condos. Within a week we had two offers on our house and found a condo that could work for us in Mountlake Terrace. By the end of the month we closed both deals. Everything fell into place as I hoped and now the money was not going to be a problem for us in going forward to opening.

The condo we were moving into was a small two-bedroom on the second floor with an outside flight of stairs leading to it. There was no garage, only a dedicated parking space. The unit was in a building that was old and worn-looking. It was far from a dream home, but it could work for the time being.

We just wanted a good roof over our heads, and the condo was actually a little closer to the Town Center than our house in Shoreline had been. My plan was for us to stay there for two or three years while the business got established. Then, after that, if things went as well as I was hoping for them to, we could look at upgrading, moving into a house again or at least a nicer condo.

When Leni was home from flying, she worked like a slave at the restaurant. She cleaned that place until it glistened. The woman was a wonder. I wasn't much help. Whatever looked good enough to me was unacceptable to her. I helped at times, but mostly I just stayed out of her way.

It came to be my job when we were there together to be more of the public relations point man. People were constantly approaching us, wanting to know what we were doing, when we were opening, anything they could find out about us. This was my strong suit. I was good at chatting people up. I was learning what these Lake Forest Park folks were all about, and I was building the anticipation for them of what we were planning to bring to their Town Center.

Moving is hell. Under any circumstances it's a hassle, but given everything we had going on, it was an epic ordeal. Leni, again, took on the brunt of the real work, just as she had in the cleaning of our restaurant. I had the excuse of going downtown to work, plus the endless appointments and meetings related to getting our restaurant started. We had much more stuff coming from a three-bedroom house than could fit into a much smaller two-bedroom condo. We had to give things away or donate them, and down-size drastically. Also, my children would no longer each have a bedroom if they stayed with us. It would be the teenager, Hannah, in a bedroom and the preteen, Kyle, sleeping on a convertible couch in the living room.

That usually wasn't much of an issue anymore. Hannah was spending less and less time with me. She was all about boys and her girlfriends. I was still hoping to entice Hannah with the prospect of working with us. I wanted to have that experience of having her there with me, helping me make it happen. I wanted it for Kyle and Echo as well, but they were too young to start out with us right away. I had a chance with Hannah, though. And she had said she wanted to, so I was planning on it.

She had only worked a couple of jobs at pizza places, so this was still going to be a novel experience for her. My hope was that it would be a special one for both of us.

CHAPTER TWENTY-FIVE
October 2004

AFTER GETTING SETTLED INTO our Mountlake Terrace condo, there was a period of relative calm. All of the initial decision-making had happened and now we were mostly waiting, waiting for all the restaurant electrical upgrades to get completed, waiting for the new restaurant wood facade work to be completed, waiting for signs and menu boards to be finished, waiting for licensing, waiting for equipment to arrive and be installed. Hurry up and wait.

I had prepared the restaurant manager at the hotel, a much younger man than me, to essentially take over most of my Oliver's duties. Replacing me was not that hard. There really wasn't much reason for me to even be hanging around anymore. I was being given as much time as I wanted to remain as yet another gift, an expression of how much I was appreciated.

There was plenty of time when I was at work to have conversations with people about what my plans were for my new barbecue restaurant. Particularly meaningful was some of the talks I had with Steve Johansson because starting his own restaurant was so near to his heart.

"The most important investment you can make is marketing. That's what the Dempseys learned from the time of the Martini Challenge to this very day and that has been critical to their success. Find ways to set yourself apart from everybody else and then put the word out. If you can hire a good marketing person who can keep your name in the press, they're worth every cent."

I couldn't afford to hire a marketing person, but I took Steve's words to heart. I would need to be that PR person in the beginning. I started writing letters to every newspaper in town, even the small community papers in the north end and as far up as Everett. I put them to the attention of the editor and asked that they be forwarded to their food critic or else the person who wrote about new restaurants opening in the area.

The letters gave my background at the Mayflower Park Hotel and the transition I was making from being "a bartender to a barbecue tender." I stressed that my roots were from Texas and my business was a family effort with help from my wife, my brother, and my sister. We would be using original recipes developed from my previous barbecue experience and family recipes. I did not elaborate that my previous barbecue experience consisted almost entirely of a one-week trip to Jackson, Tennessee and some backyard patio water smoker efforts with John Head. The family recipes were still to be determined when, and if, my sister made the trip up before we got to opening.

I sent this press release, of a sort, with the notice that I would be following up when a firm opening date was determined. My hope was to generate some reviews and if we were favorably received, then I would continue to look for new ways to keep Burney Brothers BBQ on their radar from time to time. Maybe we could do charitable events, get involved with community fairs, anything that could get our name in the press.

About the same time, I reached out to those same papers to their classified departments. I started running ads for employees, including on an internet site I had learned about that previously I hadn't heard of before. It was called Craigslist and it was a free service. I figured the price was right.

This was the scariest part of this whole stage of bringing Burney Brothers BBQ to its opening. Everything else I felt some sense of control over, that it was on myself to get something done or oversee that it was done the way I wanted. Once I placed ads for employees, I could only wait to see who showed up. When I hired at the Mayflower Park, I had the prestige of that long-established hotel enveloping me. Applicants came out regularly in no short supply.

Of course, most of the staff I worked with stayed at the hotel for years, so I wasn't hiring all that often. My track record for hiring when I was there was about fifty-fifty. I made some great hires and I picked some very unfortunate ones.

Now, I was going to be hiring people to work for me in a brand-new enterprise that I was still completely unfamiliar with. They wouldn't be showing up hoping to get hired into an established and respected hotel; it would be for my dinky, unknown, food court restaurant. I would hire them to work as cheaply as they would accept with no health benefits, sick pay, vacation pay, or even the promise of a regular schedule. Not exactly a golden opportunity.

I had talked about this part of the business with Gary in Tennessee. He indicated that what I saw in his restaurant was pretty much what I should expect, very young people with very limited prospects. He said the key to keeping them for any length of time was to keep the workplace fun in any way I could. A lot of it would be based on how they gelled as a team. If they liked each other, they would stick. If not, I would have to keep plugging in new pieces until they did. And even then, I should expect constant turnover. If I got any good ones and they stuck with me, treat them like gold. Do whatever you can to protect them and keep them loyal to being there.

On my last day at the hotel, it was easy for me to get sentimental. I never expected to have been there so many years, and a big chunk of my life transpired over that time. My daughter went from being a baby to a teenager almost ready to move into the world on her own. I lost my father and gained a son. I got married. Twice.

The cocktail waitress I started my first night shift with, whom I worked with almost daily for several years, would be there after I left. Susan Stecker was my best friend at the hotel. We were like brother and sister. Customers enjoyed teasing us that we were like an old, doting married couple. Throughout all our years working together, we never had a falling out. I don't even remember an argument. Through crazy, busy times or slow, boring ones, she was my rock.

Despite my dewy-eyed, bittersweet moments down memory lane, I had no misgivings about what I was doing. I had worked too hard and already risked and sacrificed much. There were no thoughts in me of wishing to remain at the hotel. I was ready to move on. I had given many years to the Mayflower Park and I would always appreciate all it had given me, but now I was going to do something on my own. It was time to go.

On that final day I was given a goodbye party. It was traditional at the hotel to do such things for employees or managers who had accomplished a lengthy term of service in good standing. I attended quite a few send-offs for others over the years. But I believe mine was as heartfelt as any of them. Leni was in town from flying, so I was glad she was able to be there with me.

I took in a roomful of faces all there to see me off. Co-workers, long-time vendors, even customers who had known me there for so long. I was given a beautiful framed ink drawing of the Mayflower Park Hotel, the newest one that appeared on all of their Christmas cards and in-room postcards. It was signed all around by many of those who knew me best. I was also given another framed memento, my first dollar, with the admonition to always strive for being the best.

I told a couple of stories that highlighted some of the humorous times I had experienced there and then closed by reciting a quote I had found particularly inspiring over the last weeks. It was by Johan Wolfgang von Goethe:

Whatever you can do, or dream you can, begin it. Boldness has genius, magic, and power in it.

Begin it now.

CHAPTER TWENTY-SIX
October/November 2004

THE FACADE WORK CAME in from where it had been prepared in a Ballard workshop and was installed over a period of two days. It was perfect. Ron Sher was true to his word; no vestige of Al's Diner remained. Every outer surface was covered over in rough-hewn wooden slats. Above our central counter area was a massive country-looking sign proclaiming Burney Brothers BBQ. They even put in a smoothly polished wooden bench and counter that ran the length of our storefront down to Honey Bear bakery. Behind our counter they hung a large wooden plank that our menu board could be mounted on. The place was looking like a completely new restaurant.

The equipment was arriving daily from both Jeff and Massoud. When the two Southern Pride SC 200s rolled in off the truck, I was like a proud papa looking at my new twins in the maternity ward for the first time. They were completely new. I would break them in and give them their first use. I had big hopes in those machines.

I finally met the Southern Pride rep. Jeff Winter brought Danny Sizemore along with him when the smokers came in.

"Wow," he proclaimed, "I've never seen anything like this before. A barbecue place in a bookstore. They're going to think twice about what they've done here when all those books start to smell like smoked meat."

I blanched.

"Really?" I asked with full alarm. "Do you think that will happen? Should I talk to the bookstore manager about that?"

Danny seemed stunned that I was taking him seriously.

"You should be fine. It will be under your hood system here."

He didn't realize what an insecure novice he was dealing with. I went directly and brought Robert over to have a conversation in front of Danny about any problems that we might have later if the smoke aromas lingered more excessively than anticipated. If there were going to be any potential problems down the road I wanted them out in the open and dealt with beforehand. I didn't want anyone trying to close me down later because they didn't like the smell of the place. I wanted the Southern Pride rep to directly address any concerns Robert might have.

Robert paused and looked at both Danny and me.

"Do you think it could get that bad?"

"No," Danny said flatly, "I was just making a joke. It won't be that bad."

Danny didn't make any more jokes around me. I think I might have found his joke funnier if I had ever seen one of the smokers actually operating before. At that point I had not. Danny did not know that. He didn't pay me any more visits after that.

I had another money-saving idea. I was going to need a vehicle that was suited to hauling my supplies because I was planning to start out using warehouse stores rather than paying extra to food service vendors to deliver. I wanted to use those vendors later on, but not until I knew I was successful enough to justify it.

I was driving a late-model Chevy sedan that was a comfortable and dependable ride, and I thought I could probably sell it for several thousand dollars. I was seeing used vans with "for sale" signs on them all the time, parked along a curb or sitting in a parking lot. Often, they were being offered for eight or nine hundred dollars. If I could pick up a cheap van and make it work for a few months, I could utilize the extra money from selling my car.

Once I was confident the business was sufficiently profitable, I could invest in an upgrade to a newer van.

I found an old Plymouth Voyager parked along the road in Mountlake Terrace going for nine hundred bucks. I didn't even haggle for it, just gave the guy cash. I drove it home, parked it, and pulled out the rear bench seat. I had my hauling van set. Within a few days I had my Chevy sold and some extra cash in the bank. I was feeling pretty shrewd.

The employees started showing up. The first I remember was a young woman named Chelsea, just out of high school, taking some general community college courses. She was small and cute with spiked blond hair. She had facial jewelry around her lip and in her nose. That seemed to be popular with young people at that time and I was completely baffled by it. Nothing about that seemed sexy or appealing in any way to me. I was blunt. That stuff could not be worn on the job.

Chelsea didn't object; she needed the work and my job was convenient for her. She hadn't worked with food much, only claiming to have been a waitress once for a brief period in a small diner, and, of course, like almost every female under the age of twenty-one in the Seattle area, she had been a barista in a coffee place.

That worked for me. I wanted people I could mold, who would do things the way I showed them to. I liked her personality, her self-confidence. I hired her.

Following that came another girl in her last year of high school. Olivia was dressed as a bumblebee. She explained she was going to a Halloween party on the weekend and she wanted to try out the costume before spending a whole evening in it.

"Nice choice for an interview," I commented.

"I won't wear it to work," she replied with a straight face.

How could I refuse? She might sting me.

Then came a young man in his mid-twenties dressed in checkered chef pants, which signaled to me he already had kitchen experience. Brad worked at Red Robin flipping burgers and wanted to jump on this opportunity to learn more about barbecue. He thought he might like to open his own barbecue place someday and wanted to gain some practical experience. I hired him on the spot. I was a little worried that he might question me too much about doing things my way, but he was the first one who had come that I felt would immediately work well with the meats.

There were two or three more after that, mostly high school guys in need of spending money. In every case I went with my gut, hiring them if I thought they could hang with the chaos, but still follow directions of how I wanted things done.

In all, I only had a couple I felt pretty good about. Then Riley came in.

Riley was a small, skinny, blond-headed country boy who said he worked up past Granite Falls in the foothills of the Northern Cascades. He was in his thirties, though he had a youthful look that could have passed for being in his twenties and a haggard weariness that could have made it believable for him to be in his forties. He said he had worked in restaurants all his life since his first job as a teenager. He was working a restaurant job where he was living, but said he was thinking about leaving it. He had friends in the area and he wanted to be closer to them. He figured he was going to be spending more time down this way.

He claimed to have previous experience working with barbecue; there wasn't much I could tell him about it he didn't already know. He thought it would be fun to work with a place that was just opening up. He could give me fifteen to twenty hours a week in the beginning while he made up his mind about leaving his present job or not. Later on, if things worked out, he could be interested in going full-time. If not, well, he felt he could certainly give me some valuable experience in getting the place up and running.

I jumped at it. This could be my go-to guy, my team leader. He could even teach me some things while I was getting everything started.

One of the things I had not learned from John Head or from Gary Christian was working directly with beef brisket. John had preferred to work with pork ribs when we played with the water smoker, and Tennessee was almost all about pulled pork and ribs. Gary said he usually cooked a brisket once or twice a week, but I don't remember ever seeing one come out while we were there. I asked Riley if he had worked much with brisket.

"Sure, I know all about brisket. What do you want to know?"

What I told him was that it would be nice to have someone who could lead the rest of the crew in working with meat they weren't already familiar with. What I did not tell him was that up to that point I had never sliced a brisket in my life. Riley was going to teach me how to do that.

After I had Riley firmly on board, I thought I had enough people to make a run at it. I thought he would be the anchor for me in getting this restaurant off to a solid start. What I failed to pick up about Riley was that there was another reason motivating him to avail himself to me with all his valuable experience. He was a methamphetamine addict.

SOON I WOULD BE making more trips back and forth to SeaTac airport than Leni was as a flight attendant. John Head was the first to arrive, flying in as promised to assist me with training and hold my hand as I worked with my smokers for the first few trial runs.

I hadn't told John too much about my trip to Tennessee. He was aware I had gone there and learned some techniques. He knew he wasn't really one to mentor me in the daily operation of a restaurant. He just enjoyed the process of cooking the meats, how to season them, how to tend them while they cooked. He was clear with me that he was coming back to Seattle because he wanted to give me whatever support he could so that Leni and I were successful. Any way he could help us, he would pitch in and do. It wasn't about trying to take over and dictate about the right or wrong way to do things. He wasn't coming just because it was a job and I was a client paying him. He was coming as a friend. I appreciated having his presence and his support very much.

Following shortly thereafter would be Gerry and Mike. I was excited at the prospect of working closely with Gerry in the kitchen, arriving at just how we would develop our side dishes and desserts. I already had some thoughts about how I wanted to approach that and I didn't think what I had in mind would be exactly how she wanted to do it, but I still was greatly pleased she would be with me.

Mike might be another matter. He was my brother-in-law and I loved him for being such a devoted and caring husband to my sister, but I knew that I was going to be in for days of him nosing around my restaurant telling me how Charlotte does things at Iron Works BBQ in Austin, Texas. He would tell me about the best barbecue sauce he ever had and the best brisket and the best ribs and the best baked beans and the best potato salad and the best peach cobbler and on and on in minute detail.

Oh well, it was for less than a week. And I would have my sister helping me open my restaurant. It was an acceptable trade-off.

Finally, Tom would arrive just before John Head and Gerry and Mike would all be heading home. He would spend a weekend getting all of the cash register, banking processes, and accounting procedures set. Then he would fly back home and handle all my accounting needs as needed. Most of our collaboration would be over the internet and occasionally on the phone.

And then I would be on my own. With Leni, when she wasn't flying.

I told Robert Sindelar that I was aiming at my official grand opening to be November 16. That was in two weeks.

On the way home my van broke down.

CHAPTER TWENTY-SEVEN
November 2004

I REALIZED THAT MY Plymouth Voyager was going to give me repeated problems. My money- saving scheme was not going to work if I was continually paying for repairs. But, moreover, I couldn't be sure about when it might break down. It might leave me in a rough spot if I didn't have Leni close to bail me out.

I thought my idea wasn't really that bad; I just had bad luck with it. It could still work. I saw a Dodge Caravan parked along the road with a sign asking for twelve hundred on it. That was a little more than I paid for the Voyager—maybe it was in a little better shape. I got the owner to start it up for me and took it for a test drive. It seemed like it was solid enough.

I talked him down to a thousand and made the buy. I still was way ahead in dollars that I had gotten for my Chevy. Now I owned two vans. I would dump one later, but for now I at least had an option to fall back on if one of them was giving me a problem.

John Head was with me the first time I fired up my SC 200. He had been in town with me for a couple of days helping me develop procedures. I introduced him to the employees I had, who at that point were only coming in occasionally for two-hour shifts to learn about the equipment, the menu, and to just generally become familiar with the restaurant and each other. Hannah was one of those employees and I was already feeling like I had a victory with this barbecue restaurant idea just in having her there to share it with.

The only problem was that I had higher expectations of Hannah than I did for the other inexperienced young people I hired. I expected her to care more about the job, to apply herself more energetically, to perform as a leader more quickly. And I made her feel that way too fast. I wasn't just Dad anymore; I was an over-demanding boss. That would come back to haunt me later.

John was a good role model for the employees. He was relaxed and in good spirits. He was just there to help, no pressure on him whether it went one way or another. He enjoyed having everyone crowded around him as he prepped meats with a dry rub seasoning and loaded them into the smoker. He basked in the workers' enthusiastic compliments when the meats came out of the smoker. Like a master showman, he demonstrated for them how to pull a pork, de-bone a chicken, take the thin layer of membrane off a rack of ribs. Even Riley gave John respectful attention.

But it was Riley I wanted to slice the brisket when the first one came out. I watched him studiously as he trimmed and divided it. He had a smooth ease of motion with the carving knife. He had done this kind of thing many, many times before.

The initial trials of cooking meats in the smokers went fantastically. We only needed to fine-tune the cooking time and temperature a little to give us the desired combination for when the meats would be the desired tenderness I wanted for them.

My first and most primary objective, what had led me into the entire process of wanting to open my own barbecue restaurant in the first place, was gratifyingly being fulfilled. These smokers worked like I thought they could. Load them, set them, and walk away. Come back and take out delicious, well- cooked barbecue. Was it the best? Award-winning? Probably not. OK, definitely not. But I firmly believed I would get better with it over time. And I would start out making perfectly acceptable, decent barbecue. And I would be the only place doing that in this part of the Seattle area. So far, so good.

John and I were sitting in The Commons having coffee when we were approached by a middle- aged woman in faded, worn blue jeans, scuffed-up cowboy boots, and a flannel shirt. She had false teeth, thick glasses, and a face that revealed a life lived hard. At first, I thought she might be asking us for spare change.

"I understand you're hirin'," she said, trying to puff herself up to stand taller. "I could use a job."

I didn't immediately respond.

"I'm a good worker, show up every day. Dependable. You won't be sorry you hired me."

John and I chatted with her, learning a bit of her story. She had just come into the area from living out in Eastern Washington around Spokane. She worked for a while at Gonzaga University in the student cafeteria. She certainly matched my memory of some of the cafeteria ladies I had in elementary school. She spoke glowingly of how polite and respectful all of the basketball boys were when they came through her line.

It wasn't completely clear what had brought her out to this part of the country, but she wanted to make a new start. I figured she couldn't be much worse than the bunch I already had, and I also believed I would have some attrition along the way. An extra worker wouldn't hurt. And if there was ever anybody who looked the part for working in a barbecue restaurant, it was her.

I told Martha she was hired. She became the constant burr in my saddle.

My final hire for my opening crew was there for the shortest amount of time—she only lasted a little more than a week—but she was as critical in my journey as anyone. Her name was Cindy Flagg. She was a longtime high school teacher in the Shoreline schools, mostly teaching home economics. She saw a barbecue restaurant was opening in the Town Center and just thought it would be fun to experience it. She wanted to learn about barbecue. She didn't really even care if I paid her.

I brought her on because of her maturity and her calm, comforting manner. She made me feel like I had another adult that the younger people would respect and listen to. But she turned out to be so much more than that. Cindy told me she could codify our recipes for us, our cooking schedules, anything I wanted to have prepared for filing and keeping organized.

She spent that entire week of training taking notes and then going home and typing out everything. She brought me laminated pages that were three-hole punched, ready to go into binders. She created the entire record of the beginning of Burney Brothers BBQ and everything we needed to train any new employees coming in. And then, just as suddenly as she appeared, she had to stop. She was just too busy to give us as much time as she had hoped to. But she left behind an enormous contribution to getting us started.

By the time I had Gerry in my kitchen, I knew it was too late to let her be as creative as she could be. We were too close to our opening and too many details needed to come together rapidly.

She had to be disappointed after coming all the way from Texas and taking so much care in being prepared. She brought with her recipes neatly written by hand in careful cursive. Peach cobbler, pecan pie, apple pie. Potato salad from scratch, the same for cornbread and pinto beans. She could provide me with fried okra, hush puppies, creamed corn, sweet rice. She could have me serving authentic homestyle cooking.

But I didn't trust my workers to make everything at a high standard of quality day after day. I didn't trust myself. I wanted it easy, like my smokers. I wanted something that I knew could be done routinely every day, that I could quickly plug new people into doing when I needed to.

Whatever feelings she had she kept to herself. She had come as I had asked her to. Following my wishes to help however she could, that was all that mattered.

I had shopping lists for her and Leni to go out to a warehouse store with. I sent them to get everything we would need to get our menu set, the first of many such trips. They went out over and over, in search of cleaning supplies, cornbread muffin pans, frying pans, kitchen utensils. There always seemed to be something new that we realized we didn't have yet.

Gerry took all of the commercial food service items I dictated for using and did her best to enhance their flavor with added ingredients. She punched up our baked beans out of a can, our cornbread out of a box, our potato salad out of a carton, and our coleslaw out of a bag. I filed away her dessert recipes with hopes of using them sometime later on, opting instead for pies baked commercially at the warehouse store.

My barbecue sauce consisted of pre-measured seasoning packets offered for sale in cases directly from Southern Pride. Gary used the same ones at Backyard Barbecue and they made it simple to make up sauce batches by the gallon. Simply open a packet, add water and ketchup, heat it up on a stove, and bingo-bango, you've got a sweet, tangy sauce.

However, I needed Gerry to help me create a version that was spicy. I had taken the Southern Pride sauce and just dumped in a bunch of Tabasco. Gerry tried it and said it was the only flavor she could taste. That was simply not good enough. She added peppery spices until it had the right balance of spiciness mixing with what was already sweet. The barbecue sauce was set.

The dry rub we applied to all the meats before smoking also came directly from Southern Pride. One was a dark rub for brisket and pork and the other was a more paprika and brown sugar-based poultry rub. They both came shipped in twenty-five-pound boxes. I ordered ten boxes of each to get started with.

Mike was not nearly as overbearing as I imagined he would be. He knew that it was a special collaboration for Gerry and me, a time for us to be close as brother and sister. Early on he discovered joys of his own in the fresh-baked goods of Honey Bear. He tried a lot of other items in the food court as well. Then he mostly sat out in The Commons, chatting up the retired old-timers who congregated around one of the large tables every day. He regaled them with comparisons of what he knew about the Pacific Northwest, from when he visited the area many years ago as a young man, and what he was sure they did not know about Texas. He also carried on at great length about the superior quality of Iron Works BBQ and his close relationship there with Charlotte. The locals found him highly entertaining.

The menu boards arrived and were mounted behind the counter, allowing everyone passing by to see exactly what we would be offering. It was modeled after what we had seen at Backyard Barbecue, including the slow-baked potatoes slathered with all the toppings we had seen them use and topped with the customer's choice of either brisket, pork, chicken, or turkey breast. People were looking and the anticipation was building. We would definitely attract a crowd in the beginning.

I was training the workers in the serving techniques I had observed in Tennessee. I wasn't under the gun to put things out under the pressure of serving real customers, so I could show them the way I saw the young people in Tennessee doing it in a slow and precise way.

There was a specific Styrofoam cup I had them use for molding sandwiches at a consistent weight and a specific portion measurement for each plate, each side. I showed them what I wanted plates to look like, how the items were to be arranged, what the presentation should look like.

I posted checklists for opening shifts and closing shifts. Also, cooking times and temperatures for all the meats, when they should go into the smokers. Every detail was addressed so that each employee knew what their duties were, when and how to perform them.

Some employees were trained to work with the food, prepping and serving. Others were set to operate the cash register and directly serve the customers at the counter. Hannah was one of them. I wanted her dealing with the business side more than the food. I didn't think she really had much interest in barbecue.

All of the employees were expected to pitch in with dish washing, floor mopping, and all the other dirty work that had to be done.

Now it was a matter of establishing routine by doing everything day after day. That could only come with time. My plan was that when we got to the grand opening, everyone would be clear about their job and set to execute regularly.

The cash register we started with was the one on the counter from when the place was Al's Diner. It was probably about a decade old, computerized, but with no capacity for connection to the internet. I hired a local cash register service company to reprogram it to my specifications.

That was the first thing Tom wanted to play with when he got there. We rang things up, ran reports, got familiar with what it could do and what it couldn't. It would be fine for starting out. Later on, we could get something with a push-button screen and technology that was more up-to-date.

Tom was all business in the short amount of time he was there. He was thorough, getting me set up to keep an organized record of my sales, expenses, and payroll. The plan was for me to forward everything to him and he would keep the books balanced. I was going to be just another accounting client for him; he had no desire in anything deeper than that.

I wasn't really disappointed that he didn't get swept up in enthusiasm for it all. I knew what a crazy risk I was taking. Tom and Gerry were far too practical and level-headed to get caught up in my hyper-exuberance.

If I pulled it off, if I managed to make Burney Brothers BBQ a success with demonstrable results and the need for expansion, well, then I could maybe arouse more excitement from them at some point. That was the hope I would keep clinging to.

The time had come for John Head to go home. As it turned out, having John there for the training wouldn't have been absolutely necessary. I could have gotten along without him, but having him with me as my constant ally was both comforting and encouraging.

Each day he was there he did less and less. After Gerry arrived, he mostly observed and offered opinions. He sat with Mike sometimes in The Commons talking about barbecue. He met Tom briefly.

He stayed relaxed, calm, and upbeat the whole time he was there and that in itself was a tremendous attitude for me to try and tap into. Otherwise, it was too easy to allow myself to be overcome by feelings of stress and self-doubt.

I might have been able to finish without John Head, but I would have never gotten started without him. Ed Molzan once said I was like a baby who needed to stand up before I could walk. John Head stood me up and got me walking to the point I was ready to run.

I shook his hand and thanked him, and even though we talked of trying to get together again later on, I suspected this would very likely be the last time we saw each other again.

I helped him stow his bags in the back of the Dodge Caravan. We got in and were all set to drive out to SeaTac. But the van wouldn't start. So much for my money-saving idea. I put John in a cab and gave the driver more than enough to get him to the airport. Now I had two undependable vans instead of one. I could go back and forth between them as I alternated trips to the auto repair shop, but the constant was a deep unease with both of them. Every odd sound, every unresponsive lurch, every crank of the ignition had me catching my breath, dreading another conk-out. What a dope I had been by being such a cheapskate. I would have to remedy the situation, but I just didn't have the time for it. The grand opening was barreling toward us like a runaway freight train

We attended a church service on the last day Tom and Gerry were with us. Mike found a Christian service in Mill Creek on the internet he thought seemed similar to their church in Austin. We all piled into Leni's car and drove to what turned out to be an industrial park. The church rented space in a warehouse and converted it into their sanctuary.

It was spacious, clean, and well-lit, so I saw no problem with it. There were a couple hundred chairs set up in rows facing a modest tiered platform with a single wooden pulpit. Seats to one side were for a choir of a dozen or so.

We sauntered in, saying hello to anyone who greeted us, and I led us over to some open seats in the front row. Mike lingered with the pastor, telling him about their church in Austin and what they were doing up here in Seattle helping me.

I don't remember anything about that service anymore. What the sermon was about, what hymns were sung. It was my first time at that church and I never had any reason to go back. But being there that day and the feelings that overwhelmed me are etched in my memory, never to be forgotten.

I was profoundly grateful. My brother and sister were with me. We probably had not attended a service together since I was a child, when our mother would shepherd us to the First Baptist Church. I could sense the spirit of my mother within me and all around us in that converted place of worship.

This was what I had wanted, to have this time with family, with the people who had always known me. I relished this week of having Tom and Gerry involved with me, helping me achieve something. It was what I had wanted when I came up with the idea in the first place.

And after the chain of events and happenstances that seemed to lead me like breadcrumbs through a forest of unknowns, it was so fitting that we were finishing this time together with a church service. I believed there was a higher power watching out for me, giving me help when I reached out for it, helping me find what I needed within myself to keep going, to persevere through any setbacks or disappointments. Something magical seemed to be happening. Something divine.

CHAPTER TWENTY-EIGHT

IT WAS ALMOST GO time. We were days away from our grand opening. Leni left to go flying and wouldn't be back until the weekend. She hated being away, but she had made her schedule before I settled on the day we would open. John Head had left. Tom and Gerry went back home. It was all up to me from here on out.

This was where my experience at the hotel came into play. I rallied the troops, going over all the procedures we had established, making sure each employee knew their job and was ready to go.

I started with nine employees, but had already lost two. Bumblebee girl turned out to have a problem being anywhere around the meats when they were being prepped. She would literally gag at the sight of a pork being pulled or a brisket being sliced. Olivia hadn't gotten around to telling me she was a vegetarian and overly sensitive about any thought of animals being harmed for consumption.

Cindy Flagg was a tough loss when she decided she just didn't have time to be there. I had already planned for her to be a shift leader, someone who could allow me to get away from the place and feel it was still being managed responsibly.

No one else inspired me with that type of confidence to leave the place in their hands when I wasn't there. Hannah was still too young and inexperienced. I didn't want to put that pressure on her at that point.

Martha wanted me to let her be that person, but it was all I could do just to keep her around. She butted into everybody's business, always with an opinion of how to do something better. I was having to get in between her and just about every employee at some point to settle differences. She wanted to be the lead dog on the line, handling all the food service duties. She had enough kitchen skills to do it, but her people skills left much to be desired.

Riley was already almost out the door. He had been invaluable over the training period. He had the answer to any question anyone, including myself, came up with. He had such skill; everyone copied how he set up the serving line, how he worked with meats. He was a total professional.

He just didn't always show up. Whenever he got paid, he usually wouldn't be seen again for two or three days. And he wouldn't call in or pretend to be sick. He just came in at some point looking wasted like he had been on a bender. He said it wouldn't happen again, but it did, over and over.

Martha, and then Chelsea, were the ones who tipped me to the signs of his addiction. They had seen it before in people who had been in their past, friends that went too far in their experimenting with drugs. It got to where I could see him getting antsy for a fix, just before he disappeared again for a while. I knew I wouldn't have Riley for much longer.

The one who surprised me by stepping up to be a leader by her example was Chelsea. The girl who had come to me with jewelry in her face seemed to pick up everything quickly, whether it was working with the food, the counter service, or the cash register. She always had a good attitude and high energy. She was playful, keeping things fun for everyone she worked with. I thought over time she could be someone I could depend on to lead when I wasn't there.

Everything was almost set for us to open Burney Brothers BBQ. All the equipment was in. All the menu boards and signs. The cash register was programmed and ready to go. The last thing we needed was for the health department to come in and give us the pre-opening inspection. When they issued us our permit we would be ready to go.

I had an irrational fear built up over the health department inspection. I usually wasn't even around when they came through the hotel during all the years I was there. It was automatic. I don't remember there ever being any issue, and if there was it was handled by the executive chef.

My little food-court restaurant, though, was a different matter. They would be directing all of their inquiries directly to me and I wasn't sure I had all the right answers. In my mind, I was making them up to be the all-powerful final authority. They could determine whether I could open or not. If they had a problem with anything I was doing, they could pull the plug on me at any time. When the man arrived to do the inspection my stomach was in knots.

He ambled through, testing hot and cold temperatures, asking questions about food worker permits, food handling gloves and utensils, testing bleach water for dish washing. It all seemed to go pretty routinely until he stopped at my SC200 smoker.

"What's this?"

"That's where we smoke our meats."

"When do you cook them?"

"The brisket and pork have to cook a long time at very low temperatures," I responded with some pride. "We usually have them going for fourteen or fifteen hours."

"Overnight?"

"Well, yes"

"Do you have someone here monitoring it?"

The knot in the stomach was coming back. Where was this going?

"Uh, no. Not overnight. We come in early in the morning."

"Do you have a monitoring device for the oven? Something that records and verifies that it holds the proper cooking temperature for the entire cycle?"

"I think we would know in the morning if something went wrong with it, wouldn't we?"

"That's not good enough. You need something that monitors the oven when no one is on hand to verify."

I was starting to panic. Was he going to shut me down until I got this glitch figured out?

"I'll contact the Southern Pride people right away. I can get what's needed if it's not already handled by the oven's controls. This is the first I've heard about a monitoring device being necessary."

He paused, considered for a moment, then nodded his head curtly.

"I'll let you start with it, but I'm making a note. We'll want to see this addressed."

"Absolutely. Absolutely." Jesus, the health department scared me to death. Finding a monitoring device went to the top of my to-do list and I made sure I got it done as soon as I could.

Opening day arrived. There wasn't going to be a ribbon-cutting or some kind of ceremonial pronouncement. We were just going to open. But I was as nervous as a teenager going on his first prom date. On this day, all my theory and belief about opening a barbecue restaurant in the north end was going to be borne out or not. Of course, this was only one day. There would be many more before the final verdict would be pronounced. This first day would set the tone. It would be something to launch us forward or else retreat, recover from, and try again.

I got to the store early in the morning, well before anyone else was scheduled to be there. I oversaw every detail. The meats came out of the smokers and were just as I hoped for. The employees started coming in and we got everything set up to serve lunch. As it was approaching noon, I looked around at everything and then into the eyes of my workers.

"Are we ready to do this?"

I got salutes and thumbs-up all around.

I walked over to Robert in the bookstore and told him we were ready and would be open for lunch.

"Shall I announce it?" he asked.

"That would be nice," I answered.

When I got back behind the counter at my cash register, the intercom the bookstore occasionally made announcements on crackled into use.

"Ladies and gentlemen," came Robert's voice smoothly and firmly across The Commons, "we are pleased and proud to announce that Burney Brothers BBQ is now open for business."

I heard a spattering of applause. A couple of faint cheers. One customer came up, then two more. And then the line started growing.

As I worked with the customer in front of me, the employees were careening into action. Quickly we were in a blur of activity with sandwiches, plates, baked potatoes all coming up on order tickets. Everyone was laughing, teasing, acting like it was a party.

I stayed serious, focused, wanting things to go smoothly. For that first hour I never saw less than four customers waiting to get to the counter. It was working. They were coming. We were doing it.

At some point Robert appeared close by, just checking in with me. He gave me a smile and said, "Congratulations, Mr. Burney. Well done."

In those first days I got a similar greeting from Ron Sher when he came by to try us out. I got to see my daughter, Hannah, working alongside me, excited to be a part of it all. I got to see my son, Kyle, and my stepdaughter, Echo, in line with a crowd waiting for dinner. They both wanted to have their turn to work at Burney Brothers BBQ, too.

When Leni came back from flying, she jumped right into the fray with us. We had lines, both at lunchtime and dinner, right up until the Thanksgiving break.

Everything did not always go perfectly. We had to learn a few things and make a couple of adjustments along the way. But we were off to a good start. People were coming and they were liking us. The barbecue was working.

I was happy, but I was exhausted. I put everything I had into getting to this point. Now I thought I should have been feeling like I'd just finished running a marathon, completely spent and relieved that I had completed it. It was done.

Yet, the truth was I had only begun. We had to make it happen again every day. People were judging us, deciding if they would return, if they would tell others to try us. And that would be the case over and over again each day we opened. There was no finish line to this marathon. At least not any time soon.

CHAPTER TWENTY-NINE
December 2004

THE LAKE FOREST PARK Town Center was a busy place during the holiday season. In the weeks before Christmas there were numerous events scheduled on the stage that brought hundreds of people into The Commons on a regular basis. School band concerts, celebrity author events, live music for dancing. And one of the first things people saw when they walked in was the new barbecue place at the point next to Honey Bear Bakery.

The letters I had written to the press had hit the bull's-eye. We got three reviews in the first couple of weeks we were open, all of them very favorable.

"A bookstore isn't the first place you'd think to find a barbecue joint, but there's a fine one sitting next to Third Place Books. And dang if these boys from Texas don't have it right. This wasn't purty dang good. It was darn good." - The Everett Herald.

"BBQ Comes to LFP." Native Texans bring taste of Southwest to Towne food court." The Enterprise.

"The unlikeliest spots always turn out to be the likeliest places for finding great barbecue. That's a good first argument for trying Burney Brothers BBQ." The Seattle PI.

The people continued to come steadily, with the weekends in particular being very intense.

I was at the restaurant from between eight and nine in the morning until we closed at eight or nine at night. I only got away in intervals when Leni was around to spell me. I would go home to the condo we were living in to just relax for a while, maybe try to take a nap. But I was usually too worked up to really rest. I would fret about what was going on at the restaurant and then go back in to make sure we were staying on top of things.

There were always things to do. Trips to the store for supplies, prepping, talking to people about catering, talking to vendors wanting to sell me something or who were already selling me something. Even when I did get home, the first thing I did was usually related to the restaurant. Scheduling, payroll, inventory—there was always something that demanded my attention.

We lost some employees along the way. Riley, of course, as I knew we would. He finally disappeared after getting a paycheck and a week's advance he requested from me, and I never saw him again. He didn't even call in to quit. I don't believe we could have opened nearly as smoothly as we did if he had not come on the scene. He carried me through the most important stretch when I was the most insecure about what I was doing. And I never got to thank him for it.

Two others left because they weren't getting the shifts they wanted and they couldn't stand working with Martha. She was one of the most dependable employees I had. I could depend on her to come to work not just on time, but early, every day. I could depend on her to be there and give me one hundred percent of her effort. And I could depend on her to piss off anybody who had to suffer working alongside her. I don't know how she did it.

I finally had to start scheduling Martha where she could do the least damage. She couldn't accept it and decided she had to move on. During the time she was there she helped a lot in being one of the crew that pulled her weight and then some. She gave me all she had during a chaotic beginning when I needed all I could get. I was grateful that she came to us when she did. I was also grateful when she left.

As we were becoming increasingly shorthanded, I was getting even more tense and demanding of the performance I was getting from the others. The one I was most demanding of was Hannah. If she was a couple of minutes late, she heard about it. If she didn't look like she was completely paying attention, she heard about it. If she didn't do a task exactly as I had trained her to do it, she heard about it.

Things I found myself letting others get by with were just not acceptable with Hannah. I couldn't let the others think I was coddling her, treating her special. She had to pull her weight. What I ended up doing was making her pull much more than was fair to ask.

I wanted things to go perfectly and I couldn't accept it easily when they didn't. Hannah became less enamored with Burney Brothers BBQ. She wasn't going to quit, at least not right away, but the luster of working with her father in a family business faded quickly for Hannah and her attention to its success no longer was a priority for her. She was there for the paycheck until she could make a move to something else without hurting my feelings.

Having a business I could share with family was a prime motivator for me in achieving its reality. Driving a wedge between Hannah and me by being over-demanding, and eventually driving her away from wanting to be involved, was my biggest letdown. The one do-over I wish I had.

I sold one of my crappy vans to one of the workers who cleaned tables and washed dishes for The Commons. I got about half of what I paid for it. The other one I traded in at a Chevy dealership for the last cargo van they had on the lot. It was an Astro van, brand new. It only had the two front seats; the rest of the van was open for hauling supplies in. It meant I had to take on an additional monthly payment, but at that point I was confident we were in good shape for the long haul. I wouldn't have to worry about breaking down every time I got in my van to go somewhere.

I took it to the man who did my menu boards to make up decals to put on it. It was completely white in color, so the red and black lettering he put on made it pop. I had our name and phone number on both sides and on the back, as well as slogans inviting inquiries for catering. It was going to be a rolling billboard for the business.

Being at the cash register was my usual position. I had the workers doing all the serving line work, all the prepping and dish washing in the back. For me, it was all about greeting the customers and chatting with those who stopped in to see what we were about. I was familiar with everyone who frequented The Commons on a regular basis. Just like when I worked at the hotel, I made it easy for people to engage with me, to feel I was interested in learning about who they were. I wanted us to be accepted as a part of the community.

I kept an eye on what the employees were doing. I made sure the meats went into the smoker when they were supposed to. I made sure we had what we needed in supplies. But, every day, one of the most important things I did was talk to people and build relationships.

Big Nose Vince came by many times. He always puffed himself up and told people that it was he who had shown us the place in the beginning. He had helped me find it. That was fine.

None of my old hotel gang came to see me in those early days. They were too busy, and the truth was they had moved on. I was beloved when I was there, but once I was gone, I was just part of the hotel history. There was always new people and new business to get done. They had wished me well and then I was forgotten. I completely understood.

My favorite visit in the early days came from Ed Molzan. It surprised me when he walked up because I don't think I had ever seen him when he wasn't sitting at his desk. He wasn't a lot taller standing than he had been sitting. But he still had that nasty grin.

"So, you got yourself a restaurant. Look at you."

"What can I get you, Ed? It's on the house."

"Ahhh, I can't eat so much these days. I don't want anything right now. I just wanted to see what it looked like." He looked around admiringly. "You done good. It looks nice. I got to hand it to you. So, you know how to make barbecue now, huh?"

"Yeah, I think I got it pretty good. For now, anyway."

"Well, whenever anybody comes to me that wants to start a restaurant, it'll be you I'll point them to. You proved that anything can be possible if you put your mind to it. If you're just willing to do what it takes."

"Thanks, Ed. Thanks for helping me along the way."

"Hey, a guy like you keeps things interesting for an old guy like me. I should be thanking you. Come see me from time to time. I want to know how it's going for you."

"Sure thing. When I open my second location, you'll be the first one I tell."

"Ha, ha. Yeah. Good. Just keep your eye on this one for a while, smart guy. Be patient. Things take time."

IT WAS A SATURDAY night in the middle of the holiday season and The Commons was packed. There was a band on the stage playing swing music. People were dancing. All the restaurants were busy. One of my customers in line, an attractive woman looking to be in her mid-thirties, had a question for me when it was her turn to order.

"Are you hiring?"

We were down from the number of employees we'd started with. I wasn't desperate for a new hire, but I could use a good worker if someone came along.

"I'm always hiring if the right person asks. Are you looking for a job?"

She blushed. "Oh, no! I'm a doctor. I'm not asking for myself. My husband and I are transferring to Alaska and we're unable to take our nanny with us. She's worked for us for four years now and she's great. We just love her. I hate us leaving her here without a job."

"Has she worked in a restaurant before?"

"No, I think we were her first job. But, she's very smart. She learns quickly and she is meticulous in her work. She would be a great employee for anyone."

"Well, sure, you can bring her by. I'm completely open to meeting her."

"There's just one thing. She's from Mexico. She doesn't speak English."

"Not at all?"

"My husband and I are bilingual, so it's no problem for us. She's working on her English. She's learning."

"Well, I don't speak Spanish, so..."

"Just meet her. She doesn't really need you to speak to her much in the beginning. She's very quick at picking things up."

"Sure, bring her by. I'll be happy to meet her."

"Oh, that's wonderful. Thank you."

I didn't want to disappoint the nice doctor, but I couldn't really see myself bringing on somebody who couldn't understand a word I was saying. I was pretty particular about how I wanted things done. It just didn't make much sense to me. I forgot about it. Less than a week later the doctor came back.

"Hello! Remember me?"

Standing in front of her was a tiny young woman. The doctor was not tall, but this girl, probably a teenager, only came up just past her shoulders. Beside her was another girl about the same size, but she looked to be only about eight or nine years old. Off to the side was an older man, also Hispanic, about my age or older. It was hard to determine because he looked like he had been working at hard labor his entire life. The man was probably younger than he appeared.

"This is Itzel. She's the girl I was telling you about. This is her sister, Maria. And this is their father."

She probably gave me the father's name, but I didn't hear it. I was looking at the small young woman in front of me. She didn't say a word. She stood looking unflinchingly into my eyes. She didn't smile; there was nothing about her trying to appeal to me and win me over. Her look was simply determined. It was confident. It dared me to just give her a chance.

The doctor said, "I can help Itzel with you in the beginning, get her paperwork done and whatever she needs to get started. Once I leave, her sister Maria speaks the most English in the family right now, so if you need to communicate something important you can call Maria to translate for Itzel."

Maria said nothing, just bobbed her head in agreement. I tried to imagine calling this child in order to communicate to my employee. It was laughable.

With the doctor translating, I said I could use her to work in the back doing prep work and washing dishes. We could try it out for a while and see how it goes. I explained what hours I could give her and that the job would start at minimum wage.

She didn't have any questions. Everything was acceptable. The father thanked me in Spanish, the little sister smiled at me, and Itzel gave me a firm nod of her head. I had a worker I couldn't talk to. I thought maybe that could actually be a bonus. If she could do some of the work others weren't enthusiastic about doing, maybe it could work out for a while. I didn't have much to lose in trying her out.

Over the next week going into Christmas I let her observe others for the dish washing and general cleaning, but I took it upon myself to show her how I wanted her to work with the food. I would have her stand and watch me as I prepped the different sides or seasoned the meats. As I made barbecue sauce or sliced brisket or pulled pork and chicken, she focused completely on every move I made. She watched intently, never making a sound, never changing her expression.

Usually, the second time she saw me do something she moved in closer, standing right at my elbow. Then she would start nudging me, putting her hands in, taking over. She did everything exactly as she saw me doing it. If I measured, she measured. If I put in a pinch, she did the same. Whatever she had seen me do, she replicated.

I had never in all my years at the hotel seen someone pick things up so completely and thoroughly. I didn't need to talk to this girl. I just needed her to show up every day. After she was trained, I hoped she would stick around for a while, but I didn't really expect her to last longer than it would take to find another job like she was doing for the doctor.

When we closed the books on 2004, we had been open for about six weeks. Our revenues had been so strong; I would have no problem paying back the Sound Community bank loan. We were in great shape to sail into our first full year in business.

Leni continued to work her job. She would only assist with the restaurant between trips flying. We weren't ready to put all our eggs in one basket yet. We also liked the flight benefits she had. They came in handy when we went to Denver to meet John Head and when we went to Tennessee to learn at Backyard Barbecue and see the Southern Pride plant. If she put in ten years of service, she would have those benefits for life. She wanted to leave flying with that if she could hang in there for it.

All my ambitions about doing barbecue in the north end of Seattle seemed to be bearing out as I'd hoped. I knew we weren't the best barbecue people could find, but we weren't bad. And I was confident we would get better over time.

However, what was worrisome to me was our inconsistency. There were too many dumb mistakes: forgetting something in a takeout order, putting out plates that looked sloppy, making people wait too long because their order got misplaced.

It was a challenge when we were really busy, when we had a line of customers and everything needed to happen all at once. We were dropping the ball too much. And I knew that if we were going to be successful, like multiple locations or franchising successful, we needed to get much better at meeting people's expectations. We had to be more efficient and mistake-free.

There was a long way to go to get Burney Brothers BBQ to the point I had imagined for it to be. But we were off to a good start. I just had to keep my nose to the grindstone and work as long and hard as I needed to. I was committed to making this work. It might require some sacrifice, but I was up for it.

CHAPTER THIRTY
2005–2019

MY GOAL WAS TO be in the barbecue business for five to seven years, build it up into a successful brand with multiple locations, and then sell the business to a bigger company like an Ivar's or someone else who wanted to keep growing it to the next level.

That didn't happen.

I did grow to three locations, but my timing wasn't ideal. The biggest recession since the Great Depression of the 1930s came along in 2008. The stock market crashed and sent real estate values tumbling. Money got tight. Eating out was an expense many people reduced early on.

I was working fourteen to fifteen hours almost every day. I would get up and drive to my supply warehouse when it opened at 7:00 a.m. I'd get to Lake Forest Park with the supplies and drop off what was needed, leaving the store to my employees, for many years Jaime and Jenny, to open and serve lunchtime.

Then I would get back into the Astro van and take the rest of the supplies out to Bellevue, to Crossroads Mall. I would load everything in and get the place open for serving lunch. I worked the lunch period and then left it to my employees, Laurie and Max, to carry it through dinner to closing time.

Back in the Astro van, I went back to Lake Forest Park, where Jaime had left after serving lunch to take supplies to our location in Lynnwood. After making sure that Lake Forest Park was squared away for dinner and seeing if I needed to stop at the warehouse store before going to Lynnwood,

I drove over there to take over from Jaime, working the place until closing time at 9:00 p.m.

Then I went home. That was my regular routine from 2008 through 2012.

During that time, we also participated in having a booth for barbecue sandwiches in the LFP farmer's market and the summer music festival at Chateau Ste. Michelle winery. And we catered corporate events.

Leni retired from Horizon Air after achieving ten years of service and her lifetime flight benefits. She was handling the counter full-time at Lake Forest Park. After 2008, our gross revenues were shrinking every year, but operating costs were growing. In 2011, our net income from Burney Brothers BBQ was a little over ten thousand dollars. Leni and I had many conversations about bankruptcy. We never turned on each other, but any dreams I had of building our barbecue restaurant into a successful brand died hard and permanently.

Then, in the spring of 2011, another miracle seemed to occur. Leni was minding the counter at lunchtime one day listening to a local real estate broker complain how he couldn't find a good person to hire as a rental property manager for his Shoreline office. Leni nominated herself. He was initially taken back, but then told her if she got her state-certified real estate license, he would take her on.

Leni hasn't worked in the restaurant for many years. Every single year she has been a property manager has been more successful for her than the previous one.

The bad times passed. I was able to sell my two locations in Bellevue and Lynnwood. I took a loss from what it cost me to open them, but I at least had the business back to a size I could manage and keep under control. Every year since then, our revenues at Lake Forest Park have risen, along with our profits.

My sister was right. She was afraid I would be so consumed with my own business I would never have time for family anymore. There were tough years we had to go through when I was mostly never around for my kids except when they saw me at the restaurant. Hannah came back to work in the summer when she was on break from college. Echo worked in the business almost five years until she moved over to Kingston on the Olympic Peninsula side of Puget Sound. Kyle finished high school working with us and went on to culinary school. He graduated and got himself established in the industry, but after working long enough in a kitchen, he determined that food wasn't his passion as much as he'd thought it was. He was much more interested in technology. He made the transition out of restaurants and into the world of IT management. It looks like his career path is set.

None of my children have had anything to do with Burney Brothers BBQ for years. They rarely even come by to look at it anymore. They're busy with their own lives, as they should be.

It's Dad's thing.

CHAPTER THIRTY-ONE
September 2019

IT'S BEEN A VERY busy lunch today. The tickets piled up on me a couple of times, but I'm used to handling the volume when it comes. The only thing you can do is keep your head down and stay focused on the task in front of you. Stay calm, keep working.

My attitude and confidence in serving the food during periods of high volume is in marked contrast from those days in Jackson, Tennessee all those years ago when everything was so new, so unfamiliar. Now it's all second nature.

The worker I have with me, Michael, can put out the food orders if I need him to. I will leave him alone with the place after the lunch rush, but usually I prefer to serve the plates myself when it's busy.

These days, I don't mind letting Michael be the one dealing directly with the customers. I still say hello to people, maybe engage in some light banter, but I'm not really as much into talking as I used to be. Mostly, I just pay attention to the day-to-day operation, make sure things are running smoothly.

I got better over the years than when I started. I don't use Southern Pride seasoning anymore. I developed my own dry rub mixture years ago, of mostly chili powder, salt and pepper, sugar, and some garlic and onion powder. It works great on brisket, pork, and ribs. For the chicken and turkey, I simply use a commercial brown sugar rub. After experimenting with different ingredients to replicate the Southern Pride BBQ sauce packets, I came up with a recipe I was satisfied with and we cook it up every day.

I found a chili recipe to use my leftover barbecue meats in. It was in an old Texas cookbook given to me by my Aunt Treva decades earlier. For some reason, probably because she was my favorite aunt growing up, I always held onto it. I was leafing through it, mostly finding obscure casseroles and desserts I had no interest in. The chili recipe I came across was one that allowed me to use pork, brisket, and chicken. That allowed us to re-utilize leftover meats and help food cost.

It was very spicy and truly Texan. No beans were in it, which made it well-suited to our menu. I adapted it and our chili became a unique offering that could be found nowhere except Burney Brothers BBQ in Lake Forest Park.

An older black man came up to me years ago asking if I had a job available. After hearing some of his story and how much experience with barbecue he had, I would have loved to hire him, but it was the middle of the recession and I was struggling mightily. To convince me he could be valuable to me as a worker, he asked if I knew the secret to maintaining my pork spare ribs so they would be fall-off- the-bone tender and delicious. He taught me to wrap them in plastic wrap when they came out of the smoker before covering them with aluminum foil. The plastic wrap sealed in the moisture, and the foil kept them held hot inside their own juices.

The result was that my ribs were even more delicious after being out of the oven for a day or two than when they first came out of the smoker. I always regretted not hiring that man because of my fear about the economy. He never came by looking for a job again. I never saw him or had the chance to thank him for a simple secret he gave me that made my ribs as delicious as they could be.

My two SC200 Southern Pride smokers are still my workhorses. I've had to repair them a couple of times over the years, but the boxes are so broken in I probably don't even need to add wood pellets anymore. But I still do. Applewood pellets. I smoke my brisket and pork for seventeen hours at 220 degrees. Everyday. And it comes out beautifully.

The ribs can cook nicely in four hours at 215 degrees. The chicken and turkey are more durable; they can cook in two and a half hours at 295 degrees.

Through all the years, the ups and downs, employees came and went. There were dozens of them, and so many played such critical roles while they were there. Chelsea, Bradley, Kelley, Brianna, Olivia, Chris, Zach, Will, Troy, Jeff, Spencer, Jaime, Jenny, Josie, Laurie, Alexandria, Max. There were many, many more who came through. I needed them all. They all helped make it happen day after day. I appreciate them all for having been there when they were.

Itzel is still with me.

Itzel was always there. Quiet, steady, dependable. She has been the constant, my rock that keeps everything going. Her sister, Maria, the little girl who was supposed to serve as Itzel's translator in the beginning, came to work with us at the same age Itzel had started at. The two of them work the night shifts and weekends. They both work other jobs on the weekdays. Without them I would have closed the business years ago.

They run the place on their own every bit as well as I can. Maria is great with the customers. Itzel stays mostly on the line, focused on putting out the food in an eye-appealing, consistently crafted way. She has no problem speaking English now, but she and Maria converse in Spanish when working together.

My dream of being a successful entrepreneur didn't pan out. I only succeeded in buying myself a job. And as my brother-in-law, Mike, had related from Charlotte of Iron Works when the family tried to dissuade me at South Padre Island, it was a lot of work. Oh, Lord, was it a lot of work. But it's all mine. I am my own boss. I set my own rules and make my own decisions along the way. I think my father would have been pleased.

THE RECIPES

Burney Brothers BBQ Sauce

In a three-gallon pot, add the following:

2 cups – brown sugar

2 cups – white sugar

2 tbsp – garlic powder

2 tbsp – onion powder

optional – dash of cayenne

Dissolve powders together in 2 cups of warm water, then add:

2 tbsp – lemon juice

2 tbsp – liquid smoke (hickory flavoring)

2 tbsp – apple vinegar

2 tbsp – molasses

2 tbsp – Worcestershire

2 cups maple syrup

2 cups Dr Pepper

2 No. 10 cans – ketchup

Thoroughly stir and heat over low flame until starting to simmer. Yields about 2 ½ gallons.

To make it spicy:

To one gallon of sauce add:

2 tbsp – dark chili powder

1 tbsp – cayenne

1 tbsp – red pepper powder

Douse powders thoroughly with Tabasco. Cap and shake vigorously until completely mixed.

Burney Brothers Dry Rub

4 cups – dark chili powder

2 cups – salt

2 cups – black pepper

2 cups – white sugar

½ cup – garlic powder

½ cup – onion powder

Mix thoroughly. Use liberally before cooking on beef brisket, pork butt, and pork spare ribs.

Aunt Treva's Texas Chili

In a 10-gallon pot, sear 10 lbs of ground beef; drain off excess fat.

Add four to six pounds of pork, beef brisket, pulled chicken. (These meats have already been cooked by us. At home they would either need to be slow-roasted in the oven or in a water smoker, then chilled and diced.)

Then add:

2 No. 10 cans of whole stewed tomatoes

4 cups – chopped white onion

4 cups – chopped green bell peppers

2 cups – chopped fresh parsley

1 cup – chili powder

½ cup – cayenne

½ cup – red pepper powder

1 cup – ground cumin

2 gallons – water

Cook over high flame until simmering. Lower flame and cook for 2 to 3 hours, until tomatoes are soft and can be broken up easily. Yields about 8 gallons.

Burney Brothers Baked Beans

Start with 2 No. 10 cans of Bush's Baked Beans

Pour into large mixing bowl and add:

1 cup – ketchup

¼ cup – Worcestershire

¼ cup – molasses

¼ cup – brown sugar

1 tbsp – yellow mustard

½ cup – chopped white onion

2 cups – chopped pork butt (ours has been cooked; yours will need to be)

Yields about 1 gallon.

Burney Brothers Cole Slaw

Start with a large bag of pre-chopped cabbage with shredded carrots and purple cabbage included.

Pour into a large mixing bowl and add:

1 tbsp – black pepper

1 tbsp – salt

2 tbsp – brown sugar

6 cups – commercial coleslaw dressing

Mix thoroughly and let settle for half an hour. Yields about 6 quarts.

Burney Brothers Potato Salad

Start with an 8 lb carton of commercial potato salad. We like Reser's.

In a large mixing bowl add:

2 heaping tbsp – dill pickle relish

2 heaping tbsp – yellow mustard

Mix thoroughly and chill. Yields about 6 quarts.

Burney Brothers Cornbread

Start with a 5 lb box of cornbread mix. We like Krusteaz.

In a large mixing bowl add:

6 cups – water

1 cup – cream corn

½ cup – honey

Mix thoroughly and bake at 350 degrees for 25–30 minutes.

Yields 30 Texas-sized muffins (5 muffin pans).

Burney Brothers Mac n' Cheese

Boil 4 cups macaroni. Strain and mix with:

3 cups – cheddar cheese sauce

2 cups – milk

Cover with foil and bake at 350 degrees for 20–25 minutes. Yields about 3–4 quarts.

It's not so much about making things from scratch. It's about making them fresh and with care. Be consistent. Care about quality. If you do that sincerely, customers will notice, and they will tend to come back.

WITH THANKS

MANY OF THOSE WHO were integral in making Burney Brothers BBQ a reality have been introduced and spoken of during the course of this story. There are others whom I wasn't able to incorporate, but they nonetheless were crucial in helping us along the way over the years. And then there are a couple I just have to make mention of again because I don't think the story did justice to how absolutely indispensable their contributions were.

Karen True and Sarah Phillips, for your enthusiasm in bringing us into the Lake Forest Park community and including us in so many activities you created over the years.

Sin-Wan, Michael and Rosie, and Scott, for being a gang of friends that embraced Leni and made her feel she was part of the community at the town center.

Rest in peace, Scott. The career-changing opportunity you gave Leni in 2011 made a profound impact on our lives. Thank you.

Old Jim, who always came by to visit me when he was in the neighborhood.

Ron Sher, you are a true entrepreneur. You made my BBQ dream come true.

Robert Sindelar, you always gave us your full support. Even in our darkest days you never wavered. You're a great leader.

And to the thousands and thousands of customers who we served over the years. Your good wishes and compliments have been appreciated. The desire to live up to your expectations kept us motivated to be deserving of your support and loyalty.